Robert Schnase

Wesleyan
Clergy Love Leadership Challenge
budgets **Remember**
Accountable
Prayer
Bishops **the Future** Hope
laity
committees Conference Mission Vital
delegates Justice Fruitful Change
Prayer Call to Action

Praying for
the Church and Change

Abingdon Press
Nashville

Remember the Future: Praying for the Church and Change
Copyright © 2012 by Robert Schnase
All rights reserved.

This book is printed on acid-free paper.
ISBN 978-14267-5922-2

12 13 14 15 16 17 18 19 20 21 – 10 9 8 7 6 5 4 3 2 1
MANUFACTURED IN THE UNITED STATES OF AMERICA

Contents

Introduction
How to Use This Book

Remember the Future: Praying for the Church and Change prepares leaders of congregations and conferences for courageous new conversations, strategies, and ministries. The book invites exploration, experimentation, and learning about how churches change to become more fruitful for the purposes of Christ. Each daily reflection addresses an element of our mission together as United Methodists, weaving together scriptural themes, threads from our Wesleyan heritage, and insights from the literature of organizations and leadership. The readings draw us toward renewed vision, and they cultivate hope. They prepare us to act with greater commitment and to work with more focus. They keep us attentive to the mission of Christ.

The words *remember the future* are disorienting. *Remember* points backward, *future* looks forward. Yet in every discussion, deliberation, and decision, leaders must give conscientious consideration to the future—to the future of the mission, to future generations, to future contexts, to a future with hope. Hope carries us across the threshold of "can't."[1] We must remind each other to always *remember the future!*

The United Methodist Council of Bishops has endorsed the *Call to Action* to redirect the flow of attention, energy, and resources to an intense concentration on fostering and sustaining an increase in the number of vital congregations effective in making disciples of Jesus Christ for the transformation of the world. This requires rethinking church. *Remember the Future* provides a unifying, renewing, outward-focused, and future-oriented catalyst for conversation. How do we look afresh at the mission given us in Christ, open ourselves to new ideas, explore best practices, change attitudes, and redirect our energies toward reaching new generations? Read the daily reflections in preparation for strategy retreats, long-range planning sessions, congregational consultations, or church-wide calls for prayer. The readings are numbered so that leaders and team members can covenant to read and pray over the same scriptures, devotions, and questions on the same days for four weeks.

Leadership teams, adult classes, church councils, boards of laity, conference councils, and pastoral covenant groups benefit from reading and discussing the themes together in order to understand more clearly the "why" of congregational ministry and the internal resistances and external challenges to the mission of the church.

Read thoughtfully, reflecting on your own faith journey and on Christ's ministry through your congregation. Use the questions to prompt further spiritual exploration about what you think, believe, and do. Close your time with prayer for the church, for those we have been called to serve, for your own discipleship, and for the work of Christ throughout the world.

I hope *Remember the Future: Praying for the Church and Change* provokes us to ever more robust ministry in Christ.

Yours in Christ,
Robert Schnase

1
Shouts for Joy and the Sounds of Weeping

Why do people resist change even when they know that old habits, attitudes, and systems are holding them back from doing greater good? Ronald Heifetz says people do not fear change; they fear loss.[1] People fear the grief that comes with losing what has been familiar, reliable, known. Habits, values, and attitudes—even those that are barriers to progress—are part of one's identity, and changing them challenges how we define ourselves.

Abandoning long-held patterns feels like we are being disloyal to those who created and taught the older, familiar ways to us. People hold on to ideas as a way of holding on to the persons who taught them the ideas. Change means leaving behind familiar ways and possibly experiencing uncertainty and incompetence with the new ways. Change asks people not only to redefine their identity but also to release what their role models taught them. No wonder people resist change!

Yet nearly all moments of reformation and rebirth result from people courageously embracing new attitudes and strategies. Each of us is a walking paradox when it comes to change in the church—we long for it and we resist it; we pray for it while trying to avoid any disruption to our own way of doing things. Each of us is full of good ideas about how others in the system should change—bishops, general boards, pastors, laity, seminaries, caucuses, young people, old people, annual conferences, the General Conference—and short on energy for changing ourselves or rethinking our own approaches. But true, adaptive change changes *me* and *you!*

John Wesley discovered this when he risked offering ministry in a style he personally found repugnant. In his Journal for April 2, 1739, he reports, "At four in the afternoon I submitted to be more vile, and proclaimed in the highways the glad tidings of salvation. . . ."[2] This first attempt at field-preaching caused him to leave the comfort of the traditional parish church to preach outdoors to the poor on their way to and from their labor. Rather than merely railing against the inadequate methods and passions of the established church to reach the poor, Wesley allowed himself to be changed. Wesley was a person in need of change seeking to change the church so that the church can change the world!

Ezra records the rebuilding of the temple by describing the ceremony that accompanies the laying of the new foundation, a service marked by prayers, singing, and the sound of trumpets. The people responded with shouts of praise because the foundation of the house of the Lord was laid, but many of the priests and heads of families and old people who had seen the first temple wept with a loud voice, though many shouted aloud for joy "so that the people could not distinguish the sound of the joyful shout from the sound of the people's weeping, for the people shouted so loudly that the sound was heard far away" (Ezra 3:13 NRSV).

This story captures the emotional complexity of change. Every congregation that has risked innovation to reach new people by changing worship styles or initiating outreach has discovered both the exhilaration and the grief that follows. To reach my own children and grandchildren requires offering ministry in styles and contexts that are not my preferred way. I celebrate the success of the new ways while grieving the loss of the old ways.

The Council of Bishops commissioned the most in-depth study of a major denomination ever undertaken. Based on those findings, the *Call to Action* calls for change that affects how congregations, annual conferences, general boards, and the Council do their work. The *Call to Action* asks us to redirect the resources and the flow of energy toward increasing the number of vital congregations, to reform the Council of Bishops, to streamline the work of general agencies, and to reconfigure the clergy recruitment, development, and accountability systems.

I find the directional change refreshing and invigorating. It gives me hope for a church that is more outward-focused, future-oriented, and responsive to the needs of the world around us.

And yet I feel uneasy stepping into a future without the well-known markers and predictable structures to which I've grown accustomed. Most of us who are reading this as leaders in our congregations and conferences have been the beneficiaries of the systems that need to change. Proposals for change stimulate grumbling, anger, attempts to make it go away, silent and expressed anxiety, sadness, and disorientation. People want everyone else to change but do not want significant disruption to their own area of service.

Shouts of joy and the sounds of weeping—these are the signs of change. We know things cannot continue as they have, but change requires courage. We have to pray about it, and we're going to have to talk one another into it. For the sake of the mission of Christ through our church, we need to shift focus and strategy as much as Mr. Wesley did 270 years ago.

What are the sources of loss you have experienced as your congregation has changed its way of offering the ministry of Christ? As your conference has changed? What have been the sources of joy resulting from these changes?

How does a desire for change sometimes feel disloyal to our forbears and mentors?

Have you ever experienced an "Ezra moment" (joy and weeping at the same time in the face of change)? Have you ever experienced a "Wesley moment" (successfully experimenting with a ministry you would have avoided at an earlier point in your life)?

To delve deeper, read Ezra 3:10-13.

Spirit of the living God, fall afresh on me. Help me honor the ways the church has blessed me while preparing a church able to bless people I may never know. Take me to new places in my thinking, praying, and serving. Take me where you will, Lord.

2
The Destination

"The church is not the destination any more than the plane and a successful flight are the ultimate destination on your next trip." Dr. Joy Moore, associate dean for Black Church Studies and Church Relations at Duke Divinity School, used this metaphor in her address to the 2011 World Methodist Conference in South Africa. The plane and a successful flight are indeed important, maybe essential, to reaching the destination, but they are not the end and purpose. The end is arriving at your home to be with your family or to successfully complete your business or enjoy your vacation.

The end and purpose of the church, according to Dr. Moore, is the way to salvation. If you know Dr. Moore, you realize that the phrase "the way to salvation" is no throwaway line or formulaic utterance. This is no thin theology or shallow ecclesiology. Dr. Moore uses "the way of salvation" in the full-bodied Wesleyan sense. Both the end and purpose are growing in grace and in the knowledge and love of God, serving neighbor and seeking justice, pouring our lives out in service to God. Dr. Moore holds robust notions of the purpose of the church, grounded in Scripture and derived from our Wesleyan roots. Her understanding of the purpose of the church includes all the richness of the Wesleyan acts of piety and works of mercy that you can possibly imagine!

Let me push the metaphor further. If the destination is not the church, but the way of salvation, then the test of any congregation—its worship, community life, and service ministries—is whether it takes people to the destination or not. Does our worship take us to more profound connections with God? Does it help us see the world through God's eyes? Do our service and justice ministries pull us into the fullness of Christ's compassion for a hurting world? Do they stimulate the call of God in us and provide the channels to make the difference God calls us to make? Do they take us where we need to go in our obedience to Christ, to have in us the mind that was in Christ Jesus? Do the community experiences of learning and loving together take each of us personally and all of us collectively to greater compassion, generosity, humility, and prayer than we would have ever reached on our own? Do the congregation's ministries prod me to deeper exploration of the spiritual life and the heart of God? Am I becoming a new creation in Christ because of belonging to the body of Christ in this congregation? Does our church take our world to a better place that reflects the reign of God and the peace of Christ? What is the destination and purpose of the church, and are we moving in the right direction?

I've flown on more planes than I can count, so I'm going to push Dr. Moore's metaphor even further. As with congregations, sometimes the way forward involves a tolerance for unexpected turbulence. Traveling on the plane requires me to get along with people I might otherwise not choose to sit alongside. Sometimes I'm assigned comfortable seats and other times I feel squeezed and inconvenienced, but this is all part of seeking the destination. Without the plane and the flight experience, I would never get there. Without belonging to a congregation and everything that involves—

worship, community, service—the destination of growing in the grace of Christ remains a distant desire, a philosophical abstraction.

Now I'll overwork the metaphor beyond all reason: even if I board the plane and get along with my fellow travelers, we'll just sit on the tarmac unless someone has learned how to fly the plane and has prepared a flight plan. Like planes, some congregations never leave the ground. Others circle the airport, while people enjoy the snacks but never move toward the destination. Some congregations don't take us where we need to go.

And how do seasoned travelers and flight attendants treat first-time flyers who don't know the seating charts, the protocols, and the etiquettes of airlines? Are they treated with impatience and rudeness or merely tolerated for their inexperience? Or are they offered good-humored support and encouragement and welcomed aboard?

Lovett Weems, director of The Lewis Center for Church Leadership, reminds us to ask the "so that" question about any proposed ministry, and to keep asking that question until we arrive at a substantive purpose related to our mission.[1] If we cannot do that, then we may need to rethink the proposal.

Why do we want more vital congregations? *So that* . . . The United Methodist Church survives? The numbers look better? We maintain our beautiful buildings? Our pastors have jobs? No! It's not about institutional survival. We fail if we view congregations, conferences, The United Methodist Church, our facilities, or our jobs as ends in themselves. The church is not the destination.

God uses congregations to change the human heart and to reach a hurting world. Congregations are a means of grace, a concrete and personal way God reaches into our world to work God's purposes in us and through us. They open us to the way of salvation. They bring us Christ, and through us, they bring Christ to the world. We work for more vital congregations *so that* God's plan of salvation becomes accessible, real, and visible.

The mission is not ours; it is God's. The invitation is not ours; it is Christ's. It's not about us. It's about God's mission in Christ and how we embody that in our churches, and for that it makes sense for us to work to have as many vital, effective, fruitful congregations as possible. Otherwise, we will never reach the destination.

How does God use your congregation to fulfill the purposes of Christ? How would you describe the purpose of your annual conference?

What do you think should be the destination, end, or purpose of your congregation? How well do we, as leaders, keep this clearly in focus?

Read Luke 4:16-21; Matthew 28: 16-20, and the many "I am" statements by Jesus in John (the bread, the good shepherd, the light, the gate, the resurrection, the vine, the life, the way). How do these passages help us understand the purpose God has for the church?

Consecrate our church, dear God, to your purposes. Lead us to the rediscovery of wonder, awe, peace, joy, and life that comes with being part of the body of Christ. May people see in us the presence of Christ, and may Christ reach through us a hurting world.

3

The Challenge of the Ages

Some time ago, *National Geographic* magazine included a poster of the most typical human being on earth, a composite representation that interweaves physical features of the single largest demographic niche. The single most common human being in the world is a Han Chinese male who is 28 years old! There are more 28-year-olds in the world than any other single age; the largest ethnic population on earth is Chinese; and there are slightly more male humans on our planet than females.[1]

Wouldn't it be interesting to explore a similar exercise with The United Methodist Church worldwide? What about for The United Methodist Church in the US? Or for your own congregation? How might this compare to the demographic profiles of the communities that surround our churches? The results might surprise us.

For instance, does our perception of the United Methodist family acknowledge our strong growth in Africa and the Philippines? Of the 12 million United Methodists in the world, more than 4 million live in Africa, nearly 150,000 are in the Philippines, about 80,000 are European or Eurasian, and just over 7.5 million live in the United States.

The median age of United Methodist members in the US is between 55 and 59, and women outnumber men 58% to 42%. In our US churches, we are 90.5% white, 5.8% black, 1.1% Asian, and .9% Hispanic.[2] These numbers present a sharp contrast to the demographics of most of the communities in the US that our churches seek to reach.

If the only statistic we could fully comprehend about The United Methodist Church in the US is that our median age is approaching 60 while the median age of our culture is 35, we would see with stark clarity the missional challenge we face. There is an age gap of nearly two generations between the average US United Methodist and the local mission field. And across that gap lie significant differences in perception, spirituality, musical tastes, community, life experience, use of technology, and cultural value.

A few years ago, the research of Lovett Weems and the Lewis Center for Church Leadership identified our most critical challenge: how to reach *more* people, *younger* people, and *more diverse* people.[3] Lovett has succinctly identified what it takes for us to fulfill the mission God gives us right where we live. In the US, the population is increasing, becoming younger, and becoming more diverse while the church is declining, becoming older, and struggling to reach across ethnic boundaries.

How do we reach the next generation when most of our leaders and people with authority are one or two generations removed from the people we seek to serve?

And yet there are among us many young followers of Christ who are eager to serve and lead. They are not the church of the future but the church of today, the doorway people whom we do well to listen to, to trust, and to follow. They help us *remember the future* in every conversation. Their ways are not our ways, and that's why we need to learn from them.

One of the tasks of leadership is to pass the mantle to the next generations within our congregations, conferences, and the general church. Unfortunately, this often takes the form of inviting youth and young adults to serve on committees, boards, and agencies that were formed for the purpose of the church in the past. We squeeze them into our mold, urging them to play the role we used to play and do things the way we used to do them. This is not what passing the mantle means.

Much of how we do things—our worship styles, internal squabbles, organizational structures, and approaches to ministry—seem impenetrable, archaic, and out of touch with real human need and authentic spiritual hunger. The old ways of meetings and minutes, reports and resolutions, of dividing between us and them, of lengthy processes and inaccessible procedures—these don't make sense to those simply motivated to a deeper spirituality and ready to serve a hurting world. Younger people offer a wonderfully prophetic critique of our generation.

How can we offer an ancient and true message in fresh and compelling ways? Maybe this is something we (many of us in our 50s and 60s) can't figure out on our own. Maybe this is something we learn from our younger sisters and brothers. One young pastor told me, "We have a foot in both worlds. We're stuck in the nether region, recovering from past models that don't connect while waiting for new models to emerge." We need *reverse mentoring,* an intentional process for listening to younger people who see challenges from a different perspective.

For the young among us, I pray that you let your voices be heard, that you offer your best and highest, and that you don't allow cynicism and frustration to overwhelm you. We need a church that goes where young people go and cares about what young people care about. You are a part of the picture of United Methodism, a member of the body, and we belong to you as you belong to us because we all belong to Christ. I pray for your passionate, patient, and persistent leadership.

Paul writes to Timothy, "Don't let anyone put you down because you are young. Teach believers with your life: by word, by demeanor, by love, by faith, by integrity" (1 Timothy 4:12 *THE MESSAGE).*

For the rest of us, I pray that in our leading, we find the courage to get out of the way sometimes and to balance our vision with fresh expressions of ministry.

What would a church look like that goes where young people go and cares about what young people care about? How well does your congregation do at cultivating the spiritual life and leadership of young people?

What would you estimate is the median age of those who attend your congregation, and how does this compare to the community you serve? What does this mean?

How do we unintentionally put people down because they are young?

Take another look at 1 Timothy 4:11-16 using *THE MESSAGE* for a different angle on a familiar passage.

Give us a fresh start; create us new. You are the potter, Lord, and we are the clay. Mold your church to your purpose, and make us your own. Open our hearts to love the people you place in our lives, and to set aside obstacles and ways that please ourselves rather than those you give us to serve.

Four Thousand Shalls

Gordon MacKenzie has written a delightful and compelling book on organizations titled *Orbiting the Giant Hairball.*[1] For companies (and churches!), the *Hairball* is MacKenzie's term for the accumulated procedures and policies that accrue in an organization. These are the rules, standards, guidelines, and accepted models that become established and set in stone. The "hairs" of the Hairball begin as intricate patterns of effective behavior that initially solve a problem or deal with an issue. But over time they accumulate far beyond their usefulness. Every new policy is another hair for the Hairball, and hairs are never taken away, only added. The Hairball grows enormous, until it has its own heavy mass and gravity that pulls everything into the tangled web of established rules, policies, methodologies, procedures, standards, and systems. The Hairball stifles creativity, makes change nearly impossible, robs people of spirit, limits successful innovation, slows adaptive response, and restrains individual initiative. Organizations develop large, complex hairballs over the course of decades.

Have you experienced the intransigence of an organization that is stuck in place by its own collection of rules and procedures?

Orbiting is MacKenzie's phrase for how someone relates to the corporate Hairball without being drawn into it by its powerful pull. Orbiting involves keeping a healthy distance from the deadening influence of the Hairball. Orbiting is responsible creativity, vigorously exploring options. To Orbit a Hairball is to find a place of balance to benefit from the physical, intellectual, and philosophical resources of the organization without becoming entombed in its bureaucracy. Orbiting involves a measured assertion of one's own uniqueness while keeping close enough to the gravitational field of the organization that you don't fly off into the overwhelming emptiness of space.

Hairball is policy, procedure, imperative, rigidity, and regimented similarity in how we do our work, while Orbiting is originality, initiative, experimentation, flexibility, agility, risk, and adaptation.

Sometimes our gatherings as church leaders result in enlarging and tightening the Hairball more than in encouraging greater and more creative ministry for the mission of Christ. For instance, our *Book of Discipline* grows in size and complexity with each General Conference, incorporating more and more paragraphs that begin, "The annual conference shall. . . . The congregation shall. . . . The pastor shall. . . " This limits agility and contextual creativity. There are 4,835 "shalls" in the *Book of Discipline!* Thousands of paragraphs require, direct, and limit the actions of committees, boards, conferences, councils, and congregations. Obviously, we need some standard order for the theological and corporate essentials, but do we improve and expand the mission of the church each time we mandate a requirement?

I remember one conference leader who was full of good ideas of what we should do as a conference. She said that when she stood on the floor of annual conference and looked across at all of those faces, sometimes she saw "a thousand points of 'no.'" Sometimes our systems restrain.

Congregations face the same risk as conferences when our systems foster a stifling complexity of explicit procedures and implicit protocols. Imagine a young woman who sees the devastation wrought by a tornado in a neighboring state and feels inspired to lead a congregational team to help rebuild homes. She tells her pastor that she feels called to do something. The pastor tells her that this is the work of the mission committee, and the committee only meets once each quarter, and they just met last night! So the young woman waits three months, and finally meets with the mission committee. She talks about how the team could sleep on church floors and work on the rooftops of houses damaged by the storm. The mission committee is composed of people who volunteered to attend four meetings per year, and not to climb on roofs and sleep on floors. So they tell her that this project requires further approval from the church council, and the council meets once each quarter and they just met last week! Some of our systems are not conducive to our mission. They thwart and restrain ministry rather than fostering creative response. How does an idea move through your church from inspiration to fruition and actual ministry?

Now imagine this same young woman with a calling to respond to a disaster in a neighboring state. But this time the pastor asks her to invite to a meeting the following Tuesday everyone she knows who feels called to disaster assistance. On Sunday, the pastor invites anyone else who feels God is calling them to help to come to this meeting. Ten people desiring to help people rebuild their homes and rebuild their lives gather on Tuesday.

Imagine the energy! There's eagerness, enthusiasm, and passion. These folks talk one another into bolder action. Suppose the cost for the mission project is $2,000. Is it easier to raise $2,000 from ten people who are committed to this or to change a church budget by $2,000? These ten people think of a hundred ways to raise the money because they are enthusiastic and called. Imagine if these ten take their plan to the church council, reporting that the money is pledged, the people have volunteered, and they ask for the blessing of the congregation. Everyone will say, "Go for it!" and they'll be proud of the work their church is doing to help people. This is a different system. The first is a restraining system, but the second is a permission-giving system.

Jesus challenged the rule-driven propensities of the Pharisees to model a faith "born of the Spirit" (see John 3:1-11). Wesley's greatest fear for the movement he fostered was that one day Methodists would have the "form . . . without the Spirit."[2] How can we foster systems that help us soar spiritually, and how can we develop practices that are conducive to our mission rather than restraining our mission?

How does MacKenzie's notion of an organizational Hairball help you understand some of your experiences in church leadership? How have your decisions contributed to the Hairball?

Can you think of a time when you navigated organizational restraints to offer fresh and innovative ministry? How did you do it?

For deeper consideration, read John 3:1-17.

Reach down to us where we are, Lord, and untangle us from our own rules. Help us flourish in our following of your way. Grant us patience and perseverance as we practice your love so that things that we formerly thought were impossible become real in our community of faith and in our ministry to others.

5
Praying Hands and Dirty Fingernails

John Wesley modeled acts of piety and acts of mercy, and taught that both are essential to our life in Christ. The words *piety* and *mercy* sound curiously quaint today, perhaps even stirring negative responses. *Piety* brings to mind self-righteous, sanctimonious arrogance. And no one wants to be at the mercy of anyone else. *Mercy* connotes weakness, dependence, surrender.

In Wesley's model, acts of piety had to do with the practices of prayer, worship, receiving the sacraments, fasting, and belonging to a society of Christians holding one another accountable for our growth in the knowledge and love of God. Through such practices, we cooperate with the Holy Spirit in our own growth in grace. By these means we open ourselves to the spiritual life and stay connected to Christ and to one another. Acts of piety convert the heart, turn us daily toward God, and help us receive the life-restoring work of God's grace through the Holy Spirit. Acts of piety feed our relationship with God.

Acts of mercy are ministries of compassion, service, and justice that relieve suffering, feed the hungry, visit the imprisoned, and heal the sick. These we do in obedience to Christ. We serve others for the purposes of Christ. These are the personal and daily acts of service, kindness, and sacrifice that improve the conditions of life for our neighbors. In wider measure, acts of mercy include our social witness and advocacy, our work for justice and peace, and our support of systems that protect the vulnerable and relieve suffering.

Sometimes we act as if our living in Christ and leading the church require us to emphasize piety to the exclusion of mercy or to choose ministries of mercy at the expense of congregational vitality. This presents an unhealthy and dangerous dichotomy. It forces us to ask ourselves, "Which kind of Christians are we?" Are we those who seek a deeper spirituality in the changed heart that comes through worship, sacrament, prayer, the Scriptures, and fellowship? Or those who pour ourselves out through ministries of service and justice, helping people to rebuild their lives, and offering hope to a hurting world?

Martyn Atkins, general secretary of the British Methodist Church, says, "Acts of piety and acts of mercy are like two wings of a bird; without either one, we cannot fly." There is no simple dualism. We can't evangelize hungry people without giving them food, and offering food alone never completes the task God gives us. Atkins goes on to say, "Following Christ involves praying hands and dirty fingernails."[1]

The *Call to Action* focuses on increasing the number of vital congregations. Some view this as an abandonment of social witness and ministries of mercy. However, the *Call to Action*'s description of vital congregations includes not only a focus on the means by which people grow in Christ together but also an emphasis on ministries that reach into the community and world to serve in Christ's name. We cannot separate the two. These feed each other. Every faithful and fruitful congregation practices both acts of piety and acts of mercy.

Theoretically, all United Methodists know this. But place a mix of us in a convention center for conference or put us together on a church council, and watch how we feed the false dichotomy. Social justice advocates decry an emphasis on congregations, viewing such a priority as unfaithful and as deadening to our service to a hurting world. Focusing on congregations sounds self-serving, inward-focused, and based on values derived from a success-oriented culture. And those who emphasize starting and strengthening congregations answer that without vital faith communities to reach new people and deepen the spiritual life, there will be no foundation for social witness in the future. We can do better. We cannot allow our calling to serve the world to justify an unwillingness to focus on deepening the spiritual life and witness of our congregations. And we cannot allow our calling to build up the body of Christ to blind us to God's demand for justice, peace, and healing.

Wesley had a profound interest in cultivating the spiritual life as well as feeding the hungry, serving the poor, and visiting the imprisoned. He wrote the sermon "The Scripture Way of Salvation" as well as *The Primitive Physick,* a book of medical remedies to improve physical health. He wrote prayers, prescribed sacraments, and published sermons to strengthen souls while also speaking against slavery to change society. He saw no contradiction between the care of souls and the care of bodies, and he would see no contradiction in The United Methodist Church starting and strengthening congregations while also seeking to eradicate killer diseases. Our conferences are at their best when they invigorate congregational worship, strengthen preaching, enhance youth ministries, and cultivate new faith communities while they also lead congregations to dig water wells, work with at-risk children, confront racism, and advocate for immigration reform. For us to focus on ridding the world of killer diseases does not distract congregations from their purpose; it resurrects their sense of purpose. For us to focus on starting new churches does not dull our ministries of justice; it provides them an invigorating spiritual grounding.

I hope we help one another avoid dualism and reclaim our Wesleyan roots. The mission of The United Methodist Church is to make disciples of Jesus Christ for the transformation of the world. Both elements—making disciples and transforming the world—are essential. Following Christ involves both praying hands and dirty fingernails.

How does a sustained focus on increasing the number of vital congregations affect ministries of service, mission, and justice? How does an outward-focused dedication to service, mission, and justice shape congregational strength and purpose?

How well does your congregation cultivate both ministries of piety and ministries of mercy?

For deeper exploration, read Matthew 25:31-46; Matthew 20:27-28; and Romans 14:7-8.

God, help us love the things you love and want the things you want. Get us walking in your way. Forgive us when we neglect to nourish our relationship with you, and forgive us especially for the ways we shut you out when we close the door to ministries of mercy that reach the last, the least, and the lost.

6
It Takes What It Takes

I recently listened to a podcast interview with a Catholic priest whose ministry focuses on young people involved in urban gangs. Many of the tools he uses derive from the recovery movement, including wisdom gleaned from Alcoholics Anonymous. He used a maxim that I've heard before to describe what it takes to cause someone to want to change from one kind of life to another. He said, "It takes what it takes."

This intentionally redundant saying refers to the fact that every person's journey is unique, and the experience that provokes transformation is unpredictable. A young person gets drawn deeper into the violent, chaotic, and self-destructive habits of gangs, or someone develops a pattern of drug or alcohol abuse that becomes absolutely ruinous to mind, body, soul, and relationship. Eventually, the person reaches a point that seems beyond any capability of returning. And then something happens that causes the person to want to change, to yearn for a different life more than anything in the world. That's the moment when the hard work of recovery begins.

What event sparks such a yearning, awareness, or awakening? "It takes what it takes." For one person it is reaching rock bottom, crashing and burning in a way that costs home or family. For another it is falling in love with someone, the birth of a child, becoming tired of being tired. For another it is a near-death experience or the critical illness of a loved one. A wrecked marriage, a lost job, an arrest—these events can stimulate a yearning for new life. But so can holding a newborn baby, discovering the spiritual life, a powerful and penetrating piece of music. In that moment, a person is struck by grace, and an opening occurs.

The priest went on to say that he does not try to persuade young people to leave gangs just as he has learned not to try to persuade an addict to put down a syringe or an alcoholic to set aside a bottle. "I'm not the one who saves people; God does that," he says. "I simply point to the door and say, 'I believe that if you go through that door you will live a happier life.'" The priest looks for people who are ready to change. When someone is ready to walk away from the old life and step into a new way, the priest and his team are ready to help.

I'm reminded of the prodigal son, who insistently and violently rebels against his father. In simple and suggestive terms, the Scripture says that some months later, while wallowing with the swine, "he came to himself" (see Luke 15:11-32).

People come to themselves through varied experiences. Zacchaeus needed Jesus to dine at his house when everyone else rejected him; the woman at the well required a penetratingly true conversation with a stranger; the paralyzed man beside the pool needed confrontation about his true desires for healing; a rich man needed the nightmare reminder of life without God to notice his neglect of Lazarus at the doorstep; the bleeding woman needed a touch of grace from Jesus.

How do we come to ourselves? How does God's grace break through? It takes what it takes.

I've discovered that the same is true for congregations that have experienced years of uninterrupted decline. Some continue on the path of growing older and weaker with each decade. But others turn around. They wake up. They come to themselves. They discover and embrace new life. In nearly every case, the primary vision, spiritual energy, leadership, and motivation come from the local congregation rather than from the conference or the denomination.

A conference or bishop or superintendent cannot talk a congregation into new life. The congregation has to decide it wants a different future. The congregation willingly invests the time and hard work to make it happen. The conference staff and many other clergy and lay colleagues can provide consultation, encouragement, support, and a wide range of tools once a congregation decides to change, but change cannot come from the outside.

The conference or a consultant can only point to the door and say, "When you are ready to walk away from your old ways, we will help you. We think you will be happier going through that door rather than remaining where you are."

What's the turning-point event that causes a congregation to want to change? It takes what it takes. A tornado that destroys the old building, the arrival of a new pastor, the death of a long-time matriarch, a budget crisis, a financial windfall, the loss of jobs in the community, the arrival of new families, a significant shift in the demographics of the neighborhood, the presence of children, the success of a mission initiative—any and all of these have been the occasion and inspiration for renewal in churches. It takes what it takes. And it takes openness to God's Spirit to help us change.

What's the turning-point event that causes a conference to want to change? What's the catalyst insight or experience that will cause denominational leaders to notice the reality of the church's challenges and want to change?

A number of congregations and conferences are experimenting with new ways to reach young people and to reach people with no faith experience. Leaders from diverse backgrounds, lay and clergy, are learning, exploring, and sharing best practices through writings, websites, workshops, and consultations. Their work provides an invitation to all of us. When we are ready, there's a pathway to follow. It will not be easy and not everything will work smoothly. We will have to adapt their experiences to our contexts. But when we are ready, there's a way forward.

If your church or conference has turned around, refocused its mission, and reconnected to the community and world around it in a powerful new way, what was the catalyst event that God used? If your church has not experienced such a change, what do you think it will take?

For further contemplation, read Luke 15 and the stories of the lost—a sheep distractedly nibbling its way lost, a coin that slips through the cracks among the daily clutter, and a son's willful rebellion. What do these suggest for a church losing focus or purpose?

Turn us around, Lord, and help us come to ourselves. Bring us back to the tasks you call us to—to love the people Jesus loves, to serve the way Jesus serves, and to embrace those whom Jesus embraces—so that we may find ourselves in you.

7
Forty Days

A lot can change in forty days.

I listen to the news every day, mostly on the radio as I drive. It occurs to me how much can happen in just a few weeks. The world can turn upside down.

Students connected by social media on their cell phones and computers took to the streets, and several countries in the Middle East turned it upside down in the span of a couple of months last spring.

Last Easter, the churches of Joplin, Missouri, celebrated Christ's resurrection along with communities throughout the world. Forty days later those same churches were mission stations and disaster relief centers helping people rebuild their spirits, their lives, and their homes after the devastation wrought by a tornado. Another forty days after that, plans were being laid for a new school, a new hospital, and a new future. A lot can change in forty days.

In the Old Testament, forty days of rainfall ended an era and redefined the covenant between God and the people of Israel. In only forty days, the newly liberated Hebrew people grew restless and rebellious at the foot of Mount Sinai, and in those same forty days Moses received the commandments that made us a covenant people. Elijah fasted for forty days, and in his hunger he heard a still, small voice that otherwise might have gone undetected.

Forty days can also change the course of a person's life, the direction of a human soul. Falling in love, celebrating marriage, having a baby, unexpected grief, receiving a diagnosis, going through divorce, moving away, losing a job, changing a career—periods as short as forty days can totally change the trajectory and direction of our journeys.

Forty days is the period Jesus spent wrestling temptation in the desert. I wonder how he was changed by the experience. I wonder how different his ministry might have been had he avoided the face-to-face tangle with the tempter. What was tempered out of him or hammered into him by the experience? What did he learn? What did he hear? How was he different? Did his disciples and friends notice?

Forty days is the length of time between Jesus' death and his ascension, the period during which his defeated and despairing disciples discovered his resurrection and presence among them. What convulsions of spirit did the followers of Jesus experience during that time? The redemption of Peter after his denial? The sorrow and joy of Mary and Martha and Jesus' mother? The awareness of life out of death, of resurrection out of despair? Forty days changed everything for them.

In less than forty days the direction of Paul's life was entirely reversed. While breathing threats of murder against the disciples, he was struck by grace into utter blindness. Then the scales fell from his eyes, and he dedicated himself to lifelong service to Christ. A whole lot can change in a short period of time.

Each Lenten season, United Methodists focus on the life, death, and resurrection of Jesus Christ for forty days. We offer prayers of repentance, listen for God's call, ponder afresh the offering of Christ for the world, allow ourselves to be rewoven into the body of Christ, and offer ourselves anew to follow Christ. We open ourselves to the joy of new life in Christ through the songs and celebrations of Easter. We are a people patterned by the continuing story of life victorious over death and hope more enduring than despair.

Many people reading this book are preparing to serve on long-range planning teams or to attend strategy retreats for their congregations or conferences. Some of us roll our eyes, thinking "we've done this all before." Can anything new come from our efforts? Leadership in Christ's church requires persistence and prayer, and also patience without cynicism.

Imagine what God can do in a short period of time. What will happen within our church during the next forty days? What is the change we yearn for? What is the change God desires for us? Are we willing to cooperate with the Holy Spirit in the transformation and redirection of our life as a church? Will we change course by a few degrees or redirect our energies more dramatically? The earliest disciples received the great commission during the forty days after Christ's resurrection. Will we?

I hope we emerge a stronger church, more clear about our mission and more confident about our future. I hope we become a church that is more outward-focused, future-oriented, and committed to reaching the next generation. I pray we prove ourselves willing to be changed by the Holy Spirit and redirected by the calling of Christ. I hope we break through the tangles, knots, and restraints of our inner polity and free ourselves for creative response to the needs of a broken world. I hope we are somehow different forty days from now in ways that please God and deepen our mission in Christ.

In September of 1771, a young Francis Asbury sets sail for America under the direction of Mr. Wesley. Sifting through his motivations, he records in his journal the reason for his mission. "To gain honour? No, if I know my own heart. To get money? No. I am going to live to God, and bring others so to do."[1]

I pray that during the next forty days, we open ourselves again to the restoration and pardon of God, to repentance and prayer, to the reshaping of our souls by God's grace, to the great commission, and to the spirit of holy adventure as we seek more boldly to make disciples of Jesus Christ for the transformation of the world. A lot can change in forty days.

When was a time that your life changed direction because of the events in a single 40-day period?

When was a time when your congregation's ministry and focus shifted dramatically during a short period of time?

Look again at Asbury's succinct personal mission statement. What is yours?

For stories of the days after Easter, read Matthew 28:16-20 or John 21:1-19.

Lord, help me accept the unchangeable past as a grace and to make of it a stepping stone toward a future full of life and hope. Open us to the unexpected, to the new birth you intend for us, and to the new paths we have not planned, but which nevertheless lead to you.

8
Pruning for Growth

While teaching in a congregation, I recounted Scriptures about fruitfulness: vines, branches, seedtime, harvest, soils, vineyards, trees, fruits. The Bible is replete with stories that highlight how God expects us to use what we have received to make a positive difference in the world around us. Fruitfulness points us toward the result, the impact, and the outcome of our work for God's purposes and saves us from merely congratulating ourselves on our efforts, our hard work, or our inputs. Fruitfulness reminds us to ask ourselves, "Do our ministries really change lives and transform the world?"

While I was listing agricultural metaphors, someone shouted, "Don't forget *pruning!*"

She was absolutely correct. Biblical images of branches and fruit are incomplete without pruning. What do we do with ministries that have served their time and are no longer fruitful?

Peter Drucker urges us to practice *planned abandonment.* Planned abandonment involves intentionally closing down work that no longer contributes to the mission. The purpose of any nonprofit organization is the changed life. A strategy of planned abandonment means we allow ministries that no longer shape lives in significant ways to fade from view and cease to continue, even though these ministries served the mission of the church fruitfully at an earlier time and deserve our respect and appreciation.[1]

One of the most difficult tasks of leadership is deciding what not to do. As we start new initiatives, are there also ministries we need to reduce or close down? How do we redirect staff time, volunteer energy, and financial resources toward the ministries that most help us in the current context?

A layperson told me that in his business they teach four keys for strategic planning: *more, better, different, less.* Their goal is to do more of what works well, to do better at what serves acceptably but that can be improved, to do different by welcoming new ideas, and to do less of what is not working. If it's not bearing fruit, stop doing it.

Before you accuse me of sounding harsh, listen to these words of Jesus: "I am the true vine, and my Father is the vinegrower. He removes every branch in me that bears no fruit. Every branch that bears fruit he prunes to make it bear more fruit" (John 15:1-2 NRSV). As leaders of congregations, we make decisions every day that express implicit value and direction. Practicing planned abandonment involves learning to say *No* to the things that demand our time but that are not critical to our purpose so that we can say *Yes* to the things that are essential.

Congregationally, practicing planned abandonment means ending ministries that no longer bear fruit, are no longer sustainable, or that do not serve the present context. This is difficult to do. Congregations find it easier to start new ministries than to end unfruitful ones. Streamlining to focus on our most fruitful ministries leads many congregations to rethink their governance systems, eliminate unnecessary committees, reduce the size of leadership teams, and refocus energies on ministries rather than meetings.

In our annual conferences, reducing the size and complexity of our operations is even more difficult. Most of those making decisions have been the beneficiaries of the way things are. Sometimes we feel disloyal to mentors and those who modeled ministry for us when we stop doing things that they poured themselves into. Or suggesting change feels like criticism or judgment against those who have done ministry in the form we propose to change. And sometimes we feel guilty about ending something that many people still value.

But every system, approach, and strategy that no longer serves the present context actually replaced a previous system, approach, and strategy. Endings are as essential as beginnings. Endings are just harder than beginnings.

The *Call to Action* recommends that we streamline, unify, and align our work at all levels of the denomination from congregations to general agencies. Some view this as a threat to connectionalism, and yet connectionalism existed as a distinctive quality of Methodism nearly 200 years before any general board ever existed. Connectionalism in early American Methodism involved a nationwide network of class leaders, circuit stewards, book stewards, exhorters, local preachers, circuit riders, and presiding elders. All of these sustained a way of life, formed the conditions for life-changing maturation in Christ. Our organizational systems were a means of cooperating with the Holy Spirit in our growth in grace and service to the world in Christ's name. Nearly all those innovations, which served their times so effectively, have long since ceased to be. They were replaced by other ministries that served for a different era, until they also ceased to be. Does anyone really think our current systems ought to function the same way 50 years from now as they do today? Even such immutable structures as the Council of Bishops and the Judicial Council came into being as recently as the 1930s. Like all organizational innovations, they had a time when they began, and they may have a time when they no longer serve the mission. (Please, don't tell anyone I actually said that!)

During periods of discernment and decision, such as at annual conference or in strategy retreats for congregations, our church is like a ship in the dock. We have the opportunity to carefully unload some cargo. We have time to balance the load and plan for what we need for the next part of our voyage together. We can decide strategically what to take with us and what to leave behind. If we do not take this opportunity, then when we set sail and face stormy seas, we may find ourselves tossing crates overboard willy-nilly, with no priority or sense of balance. If we don't unload some things now, we will likely unload them later in less favorable conditions. Practice planned abandonment.

When has your congregation, or your conference, successfully pruned ministries in order to focus more clearly on priorities? What made it work? What made it difficult?

Why is it so hard for a church or conference to decide to stop doing something, or to stop doing something the way it has always been done?

Explore John 15:1-11.

Help me put aside defensiveness and self-deception to look honestly at the ministries you have entrusted to our leadership for signs of fruitfulness. Lord, we pray that in you we will break fresh ground in our thinking and doing. Help us appreciate ministries that have served their time, and to imagine fresh ministries that are bold, relevant, and effective in fulfilling your callings.

9
"An Especial Care"

How did the notion of conferring together (Conference!) begin for United Methodists? John Wesley describes the first conference this way:

> In June, 1744, I desired my brother and a few other clergymen to meet me in London, to consider how we should proceed to save our own souls and those that heard us. After some time, I invited lay preachers that were in the house to meet with us. We conferred together for several days, and were much comforted and strengthened thereby. The next year I not only invited most of the traveling preachers, but several others to confer with me in Bristol. . . . this I did for many years, and all that time the term Conference meant not so much the conversations we had together, as the persons who conferred.[1]

The agenda for the first conference 268 years ago was threefold. Mr. Wesley and the Methodists conferred on "1. What to teach, 2. How to teach, and 3. What to do, that is, how to regulate our doctrine, discipline, and practice."[2]

Ever since those first gatherings, Methodism has organized

its life and ministry through conferences—church conferences, district conferences, annual conferences, jurisdictional conferences, central conferences, and general conferences. From the earliest days, a Methodist conference referred not only to the meeting and the act of conversing that took place, but to the people who gathered. The conference is you and me. Clergy and laity not only attend a conference, they are members of a conference.

According to Russell E. Richey's *The Methodist Conference in America,* early conferences comprised a family of preachers and church leaders held together by affection, common rules, a shared mission, and by a watchfulness of the members over one another.[3] They were strongly relational, providing mutual support and encouragement for pastors and congregations, and they were purpose-driven, focused on how to extend the gospel message in ever more fruitful ways. Far from merely serving an organizational or governance function (as we usually consider them today), they served as the spiritual center of Methodism. They dealt with the training and deployment of pastors, and they pooled their resources to provide for common ministries to address needs beyond the scope of any local congregation.

Conferences were times to renew commitments, to encourage ministry, to learn together and to pray together. People left conferences feeling clear about their mission, confident about their future, and connected in Christ. Wesley says that the people left feeling "comforted and strengthened thereby."

Wesley's notes from the 1747 Conference record this discussion:

"Q: How may the time of this Conference be made more eminently a time of prayer, watching, and self-denial?

A: 1. While we are in Conference, let us have an especial care to set God always before us. 2. In the intermediate hours, let us visit none but the sick, and spend all our time that remains in retirement, and 3. Let us then give ourselves unto prayer for one another, and for the blessing of God on this our labour."[4]

As people met with Mr. Wesley to "confer" together on their common ministry, he invited them to keep God front and center in their deliberations, to care for the poor and ill, and to pray for one another and for God's blessing on their work together. I love the way every moment of the time together is imbued with purpose. There are no meetings for the sake of meeting. All serves Christ.

Conference is a Wesleyan expression of the body of Christ, the notion that I belong to you and you belong to me because we both belong to Christ. Your ministry is mine, and mine is yours because we both serve Christ; and so we pray for each other, strengthen each other, watch over each other, and hold each other accountable in Christ.

United Methodists hold many diverse theological and social perspectives. We communicate the core of the mission in ways that derive from our unique contexts. We disagree about budgets, structures, and organizational strategies. We come to conference and to church council meetings with differing priorities and divergent plans for how to fulfill the mission of the church. Every local church, annual conference, general agency, and global gathering of United Methodists includes a mix of people who love Christ and desire to serve the church, but who perceive the task, purpose, and means of ministry differently. A continuing task of leadership for every United Methodist is to consider, "How do I seek to understand those who do not understand me?"

Community in Christ is persevering and resilient and eternal, binding us to one another and tying us to those who have come before and those who come after. And yet community in Christ is also fragile, something elegantly intangible and subtle, spiritual and breath-like; it requires of us great intentionality and care. The threads of grace that bind us to Christ and to one another require sustained and gentle attention by all of us. Perhaps this is what Wesley meant when he writes, "let us have *an especial care* to set God always before us," and invites us to focus on the mission of Christ and to pray for one another through all the organizational deliberations. Our mission begins in Christ and ends in Christ. Wesley also reminds us to fulfill every step of our mission in the spirit of Christ.

How has "conferring" together in the Wesleyan way strengthened you in your ministry? How does our contemporary way of holding conferences expand ministry, encourage spiritual growth, and deepen our witness, and how does it limit or discourage ministry?

How might you make church council meetings and conference gatherings "more eminently a time of prayer"?

For moving deeper, read Philippians 4:6-9 from *THE MESSAGE* by Eugene Peterson for perspectives from a well-known passage.

Dear God, you have embraced me with your unmerited, gracious, and everlasting love. Help me offer that same love to others. Widen my vision. Deepen my passion. Increase my patience. Stretch me. Push me. Bind me to others who also seek you.

10
Obedience

The Christian year provokes us to reflection upon many key words that shape our faith. During Advent, we deepen our understanding of waiting, watching, anticipation, hope, announcement. With Christmas, we explore joy, new birth, promise, and other delights. Epiphany opens our eyes to gifts, journeys, and revelation. Pentecost focuses us on Spirit, community, church, service, and mission. These are but a few of dozens of words from key moments in the Christian story that merit exploration, openness, and rethinking of our practice of faith.

Holy Week brings an abundance of words that deserve our careful reflection and response: Passover, sacrifice, passion, betrayal, serving, denial, fear, prayer, blood, cross, death. Then there are the words of Easter: joy, life, witness, resurrection.

Obedience is a word that comes into focus for me during Holy Week. In Jesus' entry into Jerusalem, in his prayer at Gethsemane, and in his submission to the cross we see a radical redefinition, expression, and invitation to obedience.

Obedience is not my favorite word in the Christian adventure. I prefer to mull over words like grace, love, charity, generosity, kindness, prayer, caring, or joy, and to reflect upon how these shape my life. There's something appealing about these other words; they pull me forward, invite me in, and provoke in me a positive curiosity. I'm attracted to them.

In contrast, words like *obedience, duty, submission* push me from behind, and they prod me into places I don't always want to go. They rob me of control, offend my sense of self, challenge my pride, and undermine my pretension. With words like these, I risk losing my independence and choice, perhaps losing something of myself to which I cling. They take the focus away from what *I want,* what *I know,* what *I desire,* where *I want to go,* and what *I will.*

Obedience invites me into an unnatural humility, a trust that is hard and deliberate. *Obedience* suggests there are some things we do, not because we want to do them, but because Jesus asks us to. Jesus commands them of us. We perform acts of grace, offer ourselves, sacrifice time and talent, express love and service because . . . well, simply because Christ tells us to. What *we* perceive we need or where *we* desire to go isn't the driving question. *Our* will is not the center. There are things we do because Jesus did them. We do things Jesus did, love the people Jesus loved, act the way Jesus acted. That's what being a follower and a disciple means. Pretty simple. Pretty hard.

Watch ballet dancers glide across the floor, their every movement both extreme and elegant. They effortlessly lift themselves on tiptoe, spinning in graceful movement to the music. One dancer lifts another overhead as if weightless, with such incredible ease of motion. Every movement perfectly coordinates in graceful patterns that make it all look so unspeakably natural, effortless, and graceful.

How do they make it look so easy? They have worked very hard. How do they make it appear effortless? They have put years of extraordinary effort into the task. Their discipline has laid a foundation for an exquisite creativity. They are able to do things they never could have imagined at an earlier stage because of a disciplined submission, an obedience to teachers and lessons and fellow students for years.

By using the metaphor of the dancer, I risk supporting a works-righteousness corruption of the message. Rather, I would suggest that through faithful obedience practiced with intentionality, the following of Christ becomes more creative, satisfying, effective, and graceful even when it takes us into places we may not want to go. In some people, obedience begins to look effortless, even natural. They have cooperated with the Holy Spirit in their own sanctification, in their own perfecting, in a way that has allowed God to use them in remarkable ways. A patterned and practiced obedience, a saying Yes to God, even when doing so stretches us into uncomfortable territory, becomes a foundation for creative and life-changing ministry.

Holy Week means many things. During worship services, meditations, sacraments, prayers, fasting, Scripture readings, youth dramas, and special musicals, we remember Jesus, open our hearts to his life and his death, and celebrate the new life given us in Christ. Between the sober reflections of Holy Week and the joyous choruses of Easter morning is a bridge, a necessary pathway. And a critical word and necessary commitment for crossing that bridge and finding that pathway is obedience. In practiced obedience is greater freedom, finer humility, more intentional serving.

Jesus says, "Follow me." The words are an invitation to an adventurous new life, and they stimulate our curiosity, our commitment, and our anticipation. But Jesus' way also includes a whole host of imperatives: Go . . . Teach . . . Pray . . . Give . . . Heal . . . Love . . . Wash . . . Forgive . . . Offer . . . Obey.

When we obey, we find ourselves moving toward those who suffer rather than turning away; we find ourselves reaching out when our tendency is to pull back; we discover ourselves offering an open hand instead of a clenched fist. We discover that giving our lives allows us to receive life, and that in losing it all, we gain more than we ever imagined. We discover that what looks like death to self really prepares us for new life in God. That's the way of Christ.

What would sustained obedience in a consistent direction, daily honoring and serving God, look like for you? What unexpected places might such an obedience to Christ's mission take you in your community?

What might sustained obedience to the mission of Christ mean for your congregation? For your conference? What tasks of discipleship trouble us? Which are we prone to avoid? How does obedience to Christ push us through to tasks we would never choose for ourselves?

Read John 12:20-27.

We give you our hands, our hearts, our hopes, Lord. Use the change in us to change others by your love. Help us follow you without falling; and when we fall, help us take the hand you offer. May your life be seen in us.

11
The Field

With binoculars in hand, I entered the field seeking a better angle to see the mix of sparrows stealthily foraging in a brush pile. The field, jointly owned and managed by the conservation department and a local farmer, had evidently lain fallow for a season. I quietly walked around the brush pile, identifying white-crowned and white-throated sparrows. After the sparrow pack moved on, I turned and faced the field.

A thought occurred to me. What if someone unexpectedly gave me this field in its current condition with the expectation that I would deliver a harvest? What would I do?

Whatever I were to do would involve a long, slow process. You cannot give me a field one day and expect that the next day I will produce bushels of corn or truckloads of pumpkins. Unless I climb a fence and steal the neighbor's corn, I will have nothing to show for some time. Starting from this point, it will take months to evidence any noticeable harvest. Cultivation takes time and the passing of seasons and requires patience without cynicism or resignation.

And since I know little about farming, I would have much learning to do. I'd want to know about my field—soil studies, agricultural studies, climate studies, water studies, and market studies.

There's no sense planting banana trees in Missouri or rice in Arizona. I'd need to learn from other farmers. I'd talk with them, watch them, ask their advice, see what works for them, and pattern my work after theirs. Yet studying and learning does not bring a harvest.

I'd get to work, doing something each day to move toward the harvest. The kind and volume of work that fill my days would differ from season to season. Sometimes the work would involve tilling the soil, enriching the soil, planting the seed at the right time. Other times involve cultivation, watering, protecting from pests and rodents and weeds. Other times require harvesting at perfect ripeness and readiness, and then immediately doing the "groundwork" for the following season.

And I'd have to attend to pacing and rhythm. Some periods require repressively long hours of urgent work and other periods involve simply reading and learning more. There are times of ripeness and readiness I dare not miss, seasons of unusual and one-time-only opportunity. Some evenings I'd need lights as I worked through the night, not because that's my preferred schedule, but because the ripeness of the crop or the changing weather requires it.

And, of course, I'd have to learn to live with mixed and inconsistent results. There are good seasons and bad, harvests that exceed expectations and others that disappoint. I'd take the long view and trust that if I repeated the right actions year after year, that harvests will come, some large, some mediocre, and some small.

Scripture is replete with images of seeds and sowers, farmers and soils, seedtime and harvest, vines and branches. The biblical writers remind us of the patience and hard work required, and of the risks of birds and rocks and weeds. They also steady our fears with the promise and hope of harvests, some thirtyfold, some sixtyfold, and some a hundredfold.

These metaphors describe our souls. We've each been given a field. Our personal work is difficult and lifelong, the risks are many, and fruitfulness is expected. How do we till and re-till the soil, plant the right seeds, protect against the weeds and pests, and offer fruit pleasing to our Lord? God's is a Spirit of assurance, of vision, of sustenance, a present help in trouble. We do not garden alone. God is the Lord of the harvest. And each of us has been given a mission field, the people who surround us, our network of friends, relatives, and strangers whom God intends to reach through us with the good news and hope of Christ.

These metaphors also speak of our congregations. How are we doing with the hard work of preparation, of cultivating the hearts and minds and souls of people? Each church has a mission field. Each has been entrusted with a unique context, the community of people that surround us, the large numbers of people who do not know Christ. The mission field includes countless people who suffer from loneliness, poverty, racism, or violence. This field provides the mission and purpose for our work, and we serve in obedience to Christ and out of love for neighbor and for God. How are we learning about this field and how best to bring forth its yield? How are we protecting, and cultivating, and caring for the mission field? The mission field includes the people in the community and around the world whom we're particularly equipped and called to reach through service or invitation.

The United Methodist Church, with millions of members, tens of thousands of churches across the continents, and hundreds of clinics and schools and billions of dollars in material resources, also has a mission field. Imagine the possibilities! Imagine the expectations God has for us! Imagine broken lives restored, communities transformed, people healed, suffering relieved, homes rebuilt, hope restored, unjust systems changed forever, souls graced by the love of God. We dare not turn our back on the responsibility given us, the mission field entrusted to us. May every ministry we initiate, every program we prune, every practice we learn, every decision we make, every prayer we offer turn us toward the mission field and toward the rich harvest God intends through us.

How does your congregation study the mission field in your context? How do you learn the practices that bring a harvest of changed lives? How is your congregation equipped to reach mission fields far from your community?

For more, pray your way through Galatians 6:7-10 or Luke 8:4-15 or Luke 10:1-17. Use *THE MESSAGE* for additional perspectives on our usual readings of these passages.

Help us never to grow weary or discouraged in seeking to love others as you have loved us, even when we cannot see the signs of change we hope for. Help me help my congregation to focus outward toward the mission field you have prepared for us, and for which you have uniquely prepared us to reach.

12
Changing Lives

"I was not trained to change peoples' lives, but to change their membership affiliations." From the first time I heard Gil Rendle say this, the truth immediately struck home and matched my own experience in ministry.

Nearly thirty years ago, I served as an intern pastor to learn the practice of ministry. A lay-led team met each Monday evening in a home to divide up index cards with the names and addresses of recent visitors to the church. Volunteers went in pairs to visit these prospective members.

As we reported back, we talked about "prospective members." We heard stories of people new to our community who held membership from United Methodist congregations in other cities, or who belonged to other denominations. The volunteer director of the Monday Visitors would carefully note membership and record attendance until it was time to talk about transfer. Very few prospects had no experience in the church. We focused on changing memberships.

The intentional follow-up placed this congregation ahead of its time. Several implicit assumptions undergirded this approach: we lived in a Christian culture where everyone had some experience in belonging to a church; our work was to support their move toward a decision about membership transfer; and, if they joined and completed a pledge card, the shaping influence of the Holy Spirit through congregational affiliation would positively impact their lives. Everyone came by transfer, and we seldom recorded a profession of faith.

When I graduated from seminary, I patterned my own practices accordingly. I remember countless visits to the homes of prospective members on Sunday evenings. We delivered bread or plants. We provided literature about our ministries and welcomed people. My focus was still directed at membership affiliations.

As we reached more young adults, we discovered that many had never belonged to a church, and neither had their parents before them. There was no membership to transfer!

People entered into our community of faith, not desiring to change their membership, but to be shaped by our ministries. They'd sing with the choir, serve on a Habitat for Humanity-type project, or sign up for a Bible study. We created a low threshold for entry into our ministries while developing a higher-threshold understanding of membership.

While we didn't call it that at the time, we created a robust discipling system. Nearly two hundred people worked through *DISCIPLE Bible Study,* and more than two hundred attended Emmaus weekends. Nearly two hundred offered themselves to hands-on mission projects, and through lay-coordinated Consecration Sundays, we developed a pool of people who became articulate about expressing how giving related to their spiritual life. Most of our core leaders experienced all four of these life-changing ministries. Our most visionary new ministries resulted from the committed, spiritually mature leaders who were formed by these experiences. Lives were changed, and through them God changed the community and world around us.

What do we really hope happens because someone belongs to a United Methodist congregation? What's the end and purpose we pray for? What does the church exist to do?

Belonging to the body of Christ, with time, mysteriously causes us to become a different person, with more depth, peace, and courage. We become more hopeful, more thankful, less reactive, gentler, more patient, more resilient, less angry, better able to relate. We attend to others with greater compassion. We more readily offer ourselves in service to God and neighbor. We care for those whom we may formerly have overlooked. We grow in grace, and in the knowledge and love of God. Sometimes the differences are nuanced and the progress seems imperceptibly slow, like someone taking yoga classes who appears the same from the outside, but who has developed within them a greater flexibility, smoother breathing, and increased circulation. The change is real, but hardly discernible to other people. Other times, the change noticeably reshapes outward behaviors. Slow or fast, unrevealed or dramatic—God uses our belonging to the body of Christ to change us from the inside out.

Gil Rendle suggests that vibrant organizations "must learn to be *steady in purpose but flexible in strategy.*" Long-established congregations and conferences risk becoming so steady in strategy that they lose focus of their purpose.[1]

Many of our churches still operate on assumptions from a previous era, and they hold to strategies that no longer work. We expect good Christians to move into our communities, visit our Sunday services, and want to join. But most people around us are seeking something other than membership; they are seeking authentic community, profound purpose, a deeper spirituality, and ways to make a difference with their lives. They are seeking the changed life that comes through belonging to Christ.

The *Call to Action* invites us to intentionally focus on the mission and impact of our local church ministries. *Intentional* means having a plan in mind. It refers to our determination to having a purpose to what we do and to developing the right strategies to support the purpose. *Intentional* derives from Latin words meaning "to stretch out for, to aim at." Intentional ratchets up commitment and consistency of effort.

God uses congregations to change peoples' lives, and through changed lives, God changes the world. That's a purpose worth preserving, even if we have to change our strategies.

How would you express the purpose of your congregation? What do you hope happens because someone enters into the life of your church? How does God use your congregation to change lives? To change the world?

Which ministries of your conference help congregations lead people to active faith in Christ?

For further focus, reflect on several stories of Jesus that come immediately to mind, and consider how lives are changed by his presence. Or read Romans 12:1-3 from *THE MESSAGE* for a refreshing interpretation of a favorite passage.

Help me, O God, to offer my gifts and talents to your service in such a way that our congregation may be a place where people of all ages grow in grace and in the knowledge and love of your word. Help us open the doors of our hearts to you as we open the doors of our church to others.

13
Fruit

While visiting a large, wealthy congregation, I asked the leaders to tell me about their youth ministry. They immediately told me that they believe they have the finest youth ministry in the state. They gave me a tour of the youth rooms that had recently been remodeled with fine furnishings, flat screen TVs, and several special game areas. Then they showed me the two new vans that had been donated to the church for the youth. They expressed great satisfaction with the high-quality youth director whom they had hired a few weeks earlier after an extensive search. They talked about the excellent volunteers and youth sponsors who support the ministry, and they even said that they had set aside a generous discretionary fund in the budget so that the youth ministry would never have to worry about resources. They ended by saying, "So now you see why we believe we have the best youth ministry in the state."

Have you noticed anything missing in this description? What about the *youth?* When I asked about the youth, they told me they had about eight young people who participated in the youth ministry at their church.

Vines, branches, seeds, vineyards, soils, farmers, fig trees, harvests, sowers, weeds, roots. Throughout Scripture, fruitfulness provides a metaphor of many profound aspects of the spiritual life and of ministry. Jesus uses fruitfulness to draw our attention to the impact, the consequences, the results of our life in Christ and our ministry for Christ. *Fruit* refers to what Christ accomplishes in us and through us. *Fruitless* means inconsequential, ineffective, showing no result. Jesus says, "My father is glorified by this, that you bear much fruit and become my disciples" (John 15:8 NRSV). Fruit evidences discipleship; following Jesus and fruitfulness are inextricably linked. Disciples bear fruit.

How do we identify the fruit of youth ministry? First, we actually count the number of youth we are reaching. How many young people attend, serve, engage, or participate? Second, we look at the change of life that actually takes place because of their participation. What is the change that happens in the life of a young person because of this ministry? Are they learning to become more compassionate, to engage the spiritual life, to pray, to serve, and to follow Christ? Are they developing the habits that lead to a life of faith? These are the fruits of youth ministry: the numbers of youth reached and the change of heart and of life that comes with that. All of the other things—the facilities, the vans, the budget, even the volunteers and the leadership—are input rather than outcomes. When we are unclear about our purpose as an organization, we fall into the pattern of measuring input rather than outcomes. We start measuring how much time we spend on something, how much money we have spent on it, and how many people are working on it without looking at what the results are. Nonprofit organizations are especially prone to that.

Vibrant, fruitful, growing congregations focus on fruitfulness. They draw their attention toward impact and results. They measure and learn from their results, and they refine their approaches to increase fruitfulness. If a ministry bears no fruit, they stop doing it. They redirect resources toward other means of reaching people or changing lives.

Some elements of ministry are simply immeasurable. But the fact that there are some things in ministry that cannot be measured does not stop us from the need to focus on fruitfulness and impact rather than input. Where we can measure, we count those things that matter, but where we cannot measure, we learn to describe what the fruit is.

I was visiting a congregation when someone approached me to tell the story of how that church had changed her life. Three years before she had been driving by the church on a Sunday morning. Something about the sermon description on the church sign struck her attention. She had not left home with any intention to attend church. But she drove into the parking lot, and visited worship. She found herself surrounded by people who received her and embraced her and sustained her. Soon she became a regular attendee, and joined a Bible study. She told me she learned to sing again. A few months before my visit to the church, her husband died. She told me that she could not have survived without the people of that church and without the embrace of Christ through that community of faith.

How do you measure something like that? The change in her life is the fruit of a dynamic ministry, but no metric can capture the kind of experience that she had. Some aspects of ministry are intrinsically immeasurable, and yet we have to focus on fruitfulness and draw our attention toward outcomes rather than input. There are some things that we measure to evaluate fruitfulness, and there are other things that are immeasurable, which we learn how to describe and bear witness to.

What are some of the most visible fruits of your own personal ministry? How has God used you to change the lives of other people?

How would you measure or describe the fruitfulness of some of your most vital ministries? Your worship? Your youth ministry? Your mission and outreach? Your social witness?

Read John 15:1-14.

Ripen in us the expectation of serving you fruitfully. Save us from arrogant self-congratulations, and help us honestly seek to view our ministry through your eyes. May your love become real in us, and your kingdom become visible through us.

14
People No One Else Can Reach

I would not be a Christian today if it were not for The United Methodist Church.

That's a rather bold statement. I've only recently come to realize this as I reflect on the formative events of my early discipleship. If not for the particular approach to theology and practice expressed in The United Methodist Church, I would likely have followed a path of rejecting faith.

I remember an experience that followed the 1972 earthquake in Nicaragua that killed more than 5,000. I was 15 years old, and several of my friends were active in a charismatic Christian house group. They were reading *The Late Great Planet Earth* about signs of the end times. I saw an adult leader clap her hands and praise God for the earthquake because it was a sign that we were one step closer to the end! I was outraged. I was so furious about "Christianity" that I told my pastor I could no longer be a Christian if that's what Christians believe. He patiently listened and offered alternative views of those obscure apocalyptic passages. He spoke of God's grace and talked about what our church was doing for the people of Nicaragua and how I could help. If the only expression of Christianity open to me at that age had been that group of friends, I would not be a Christian today.

That was one of several experiences that opened the door to the spiritual life when other doors closed to me. My girlfriend was active in a fundamentalist Baptist church. The role of women and the attitude toward women that she accepted offended my common sense even before it contradicted my biblical understanding. At our United Methodist church, women chaired committees and taught from the pulpit, and I could not imagine belonging to a community that excluded women. Later, a classmate committed suicide. Hundreds of students attended the funeral in a fundamentalist church where the pastor spoke about how we should all feel happy because Martin was in a better place. He told us not to cry, because God has a reason for everything he does. He suggested that Martin had done things that caused God to do this. The image of a punitive God who causes suffering and the inability of the pastor to address the real grief in the room made me cringe. The experience sent me back to my pastor. If this was Christianity, I wanted no part of it. A month later, Martin's father killed himself.

There were branches of the Christian family that surrounded me as a teenager that were militantly anti-science and anti-intellectual, and that forced people to choose between the Bible and evolution as if these were fundamentally incompatible. I could not have followed Christ if it meant giving up my intellectual curiosity. There were branches that were perfunctory in their liturgy, void of music and song, and entirely intellectual in their approaches, and the emptiness left me cold. Some of my friends were strict Nazarenes, and they could not go to movies, watch TV, or attend plays. Their isolation from society would not reach me. There were denominational families that prohibited birth control, and these made no sense to me. And there were churches that railed against gays and lesbians in hateful and hurtful ways, and I could not belong to a community like that. There are many theological disagreements and clashing perspectives in The United Methodist Church about homosexuality, but I'm glad to belong to a church that does not avoid the hard conversations and the complex issues. Sincere people of faith strongly disagree, but I'm glad we say that homosexuals are people of sacred worth, loved by God like every person on earth.

United Methodism's theology of grace, varieties of worship, emphasis on inner holiness and social witness, global vision, hymnody, our ability to hold together head and heart, our respect for women and men, our openness to people of all nations and ethnicities, our vision to transform the world through audacious projects like Imagine No Malaria—these form an expression of Christianity, a way of following Jesus, that can reach people that no other faith expression is able to reach. I'm not saying our approach is better than all the others; I'm merely suggesting that people respond to the truth of Christ through our expression of faith who cannot respond to other expressions. This form of faith and practice reached me, and without The United Methodist Church I suspect I would never have become a Christian.

The goal of rethinking our practices and changing our attitudes and revitalizing our churches is not to save the denomination or the institutions of the church. I'm offended by those who accuse people involved in leading change of merely working for institutional survival. I have poured thirty years into the work of ministry in Christ's name, and I have not done this to maintain an institution.

The reason I pour myself into the ministry and into leading the church comes from a deep-rooted place inside. It is grounded in the grace I have experienced, an initiating love that sought and found me through countless people who brought me God's unconditional love. This desire to share God's grace is God-given and sacred.

From the depths of my soul, I desire for people to love and be loved, to experience a sense of purpose from serving others, and to believe that their lives matter. I want people to feel immersed in community, surrounded and sustained. I genuinely desire for them to discover the inner life, and to learn to ease the suffering that comes with empty strivings. I want them to discover that love is the better way, and that the ultimate expression of love can be discovered in Christ. The spiritual life changes us, and through us God's Spirit changes the lives of those around us. Patterns of violence and injustice can be interrupted, loneliness can be overcome and suffering relieved, and there is a depth to life that is sacred and worthy of cultivation.

There are people who can receive the love of God in the form we offer it who otherwise would never be able to do so. Methodism began as a way of life, and this way of life, deep-rooted in our theology and practice, is worthy of fostering, not for our sake, but for the love of God in Christ.

In *Leading Beyond the Walls: Developing Congregations with a Heart for the Unchurched,* **Adam Hamilton suggests that every church leader should be able to answer the following questions: Why do people need Christ? Why do people need the church? Why do people need The United Methodist Church?[1]**

What elements of our faith and practice form a way of following Jesus that made The UMC the way for God to reach you? What makes it worth the effort to strengthen the United Methodist witness?

For Scriptural exploration, read Luke 5:36-39.

Thank you, Lord, for the people and ministries you have used to reach us. Thank you for your love that would not let go of us and for your grace that searched for us and sought us through friends, family, and strangers. Now cause us to be what you call us to be: disciples, ambassadors, and servants in the world.

15
Love With Legs

John Wesley's *inner holiness,* the sanctifying and perfecting love at work inside us, finds outward expression in *social witness,* a dedicated commitment to changing conditions that rob people of fullness of life. Social witness serves God, who is the "lover of justice" (Psalm 99:4 NRSV). United Methodists perceive God's activity not merely in stories of personal transformation but in the great shifts of history toward justice, release from oppression, and relief from suffering.

Whenever United Methodists gather in conference, they focus not only on how God uses faith communities to reshape human souls but also on how God works through the church to affect society. Disciples place themselves in service to God "for the transformation of the world." Many people feel that the church should avoid controversial issues. But while conscientious Christians may seriously disagree about social and legislative strategies to feed the hungry, heal the sick, protect the innocent, and foster peace, no Christian can act as if these things do not matter to God. How should disciples of Jesus respond?

"Justice is love with legs," one seminary professor said. God's love takes a social form, a political expression, when the followers of Jesus learn to love strangers by relieving suffering though programs to prevent disease, health care systems that serve the poor as well as the wealthy, and laws that protect people from injustice.

Victims of violence, poverty, and discrimination, and people who suffer through war, famine, or natural disaster often lack the power to effect change that will transform their circumstances. If no one with power and resources speaks for them, how can their voices be heard? To *advocate* means to speak for, to act on behalf of, to give support. Among the most important ways followers of Christ express God's gracious love is by speaking up for children, the oppressed, the homeless, the poor, or the marginalized who cannot speak for themselves.

As followers of Jesus, we look at the world from the perspective of someone who suffered innocently—a person who was crushed and broken by the world's powers—rather than through the lens of privilege, power, and wealth. Christianity began with catastrophic brokenness and violence, resulting in a persevering, sacrificial love that drives us to work on behalf of the suffering with unending passion. We can do no other.

Some social witness the world understands—seeking cures to diseases, protecting children from abuse, supporting victims of violence. Other forms of social witness the world cannot fathom because the ideas run counter to deep cultural biases or because such initiatives seem foolish, unrealistic, or hopeless—working with violent offenders, protesting torture, organizing for peace, protecting the rights of immigrants.

Prophetic voices help us see the incongruity between what we believe and the personal choices we actually make. The dissonance is uncomfortable. We want such voices to be wrong, even when we intuitively know that some of what they say is true. Listening attentively rather than reacting with indignation may cause us to rethink and to act with greater fairness and more compassion. We are able to influence systems and make personal choices that align more truly with the deep principles we hold and with the scriptural witness we have inherited. God speaks to us sometimes through the voices of people who disagree with us just as the prophets of the Old Testament bothered the comfortable and complacent in days gone by. They rally us to a collective sense of responsibility.

John Wesley writes that "Christianity is essentially a social religion; and that to turn it into a solitary religion, is indeed to destroy it."[1] He calls us to immerse ourselves in the world and not to separate ourselves from it. Without immersing ourselves in the world, we cannot influence the lives of others or become the force for good that God desires us to become.

The United Methodist *Call to Action* urges us "to redirect the flow of attention, energy, and resources to an intense concentration on fostering and sustaining an increase in the number of vital congregations effective in making disciples of Jesus Christ for the transformation of the world."[2]

Does this mean we neglect our social witness as United Methodists? I cannot imagine The United Methodist Church without a robust engagement with the world. Begin with the end in mind: the transformation of the world and the reign of God that we see revealed in the life, death, and resurrection of Christ.

God works through us and through communities of faith to transform the world. The more we cooperate with the Holy Spirit in forming disciples who are mature in faith and committed to service, the greater our social witness.

We are personal disciples and social creatures, and God's grace leads us to private action and public change. God forms us in the way of Christ not merely for our own personal benefit but for the transformation of the world. *How do we have in us the mind that was in Christ Jesus?* is a social question as well as a personal one.

How does your ministry reveal God's passion for justice? When was a time you offered a ministry of advocacy on behalf of those who had no power to do so themselves? Does your congregation offer a social witness? How do you evaluate its effectiveness?

When has someone's prophetic voice provoked you to positive ministry despite your initial resistance? What role do you think the church should play in social change? What role do you think annual and general conferences should play?

For scriptural study, read Eugene Peterson's interpretation of Matthew 5:13-16 in *THE MESSAGE* for a fresh restatement of a common passage, or see Amos 5:21-24.

Give us obedient hearts, Lord, to do those things we know you call us to do but which we nevertheless neglect or ignore. Open our hearts that we may see people as Jesus sees them, and see Jesus in the people we serve. Make us attentive to those society overlooks, and courageous in your causes of justice, mercy, and peace.

16
Every Dollar Has a Mission

Apportionment formulas, budget requests, salaries, pensions, line items, giving patterns, reserves, expenditures, capital costs, stewardship, reductions, audits, revenue projections . . . welcome to the vocabulary of church finances! This is the language we use to navigate and deliberate the fiscal aspects of our mission at congregational, conference, and general church levels. Understanding the nuances of church finance and aligning our resources with our mission is a daunting task.

Every single dollar spent by a congregation or conference was first placed in an offering plate and offered up to God. Multimillion dollar budgets begin as coins from children, folded bills stuck in envelopes by young families, and checks written by retirees. Each dollar has been voluntarily contributed by someone following the promptings of the Spirit, and each has been prayed over by a pastor during worship and counted by a church treasurer and deliberated over by congregational leaders seeking to fulfill the mission of Christ. Each dollar has been sent on a mission.

As a pastor and as a bishop, I've remained keenly aware that every financial resource and expenditure I oversee comes from the generosity of people seeking to serve God faithfully, and this has made me conscientious to a fault when we make decisions about money. Does this use of money honor God? Does it further the mission of the church? Do donors feel well served?

In a large, complex, multitiered organization like The United Methodist Church, the distance between the people who offer their gifts to God during worship and the ultimate decision about how some portion of those gifts will be used grows with each layer of ministry. If leaders become too disconnected from the original giving, they risk losing sight of the spiritual meaning and missional intent that the money represents. "It only costs a thousand dollars" in the congregation's finance committee becomes "It's only ten thousand dollars" in annual conference discussions, and this leads to "It only costs a few hundred thousand dollars" at General Conference.

Jesus notices the woman who drops two coins in the temple treasury, declaring that she has given more than all the others because she, out of her poverty, gave everything she had. Her two coins make no noticeable impact on the temple budget, but Jesus perceives the sacred and sacrificial quality of her gift. God uses her gift to reconfigure her interior life, to reshape her character and spirit. The gift represents an element of her love for God and her desire to further God's purposes. It's not merely about what she does, but about what she becomes through the gift, a person of remarkable generosity and largeness of heart. She grows in the image of God.

Usually we think of this story as contrasting the size of her gift with the offerings of the wealthy. As we lead our congregations and conferences, let's think of the story another way. How do you suppose the two coins were used by those who had responsibility for the treasury? Merely to enrich self-serving religious leaders? Were they lost in the vast treasury of funds or wasted for extraneous and unimportant expenses? Were the coins mixed in with all the other gifts to cover the costs for the oil burning in the lamps that lit the temple? Were they distributed to the poor to help someone in even more dire need than the widow herself? In short, were the coins used in a manner that truly honored the spiritual depth and personal sacrifice of the donor?

The Towers Watson study of our denomination, which serves as the foundation of the *Call to Action*, teaches us much. One of the most remarkable patterns the study revealed is how rapidly our costs for operating congregations, conferences, and general church ministries have increased during the same period that our membership and attendance in the United States have precipitously declined. Per capita giving (average annual donation per member) and per capita debt (amount of local church debt per member) have increased year after year for decades. Giving goes up while attendance goes down. Annual budgets for churches are up while the people to cover those costs become fewer and older. While we honor the great generosity that has sustained these models of ministry for so long, we also realize that the overall trend makes these models fundamentally unsustainable into the future.

Congregational leaders and conference delegates carry an immense responsibility. They make decisions that have huge consequences for local congregations, for seminaries, for attempts to eradicate malaria, for initiatives to reach young people, and for infrastructures that support disaster relief. The numbers are significant over which leaders regularly pray and deliberate. Many of our most robust congregations, along with our denomination, operate with an expansive vision and extensive responsibilities. But we can never allow the size and complexity of the task to distract us from our responsibility to align money with the mission of the church. After all, it's not our money; it's God's. It's not our mission; it's Christ's. It's not merely dollars and cents; it's the faithful offering of children, young adults, families, and the elderly from all walks of life.

How does the fact that the money we discuss at church councils and conferences derives from the offerings of people to God in worship shape your decision-making about budgets?

What values do you think should drive financial decisions for church leaders? How should money relate to, shape, or serve the mission? How well do you feel your congregation and conference do with prioritizing and aligning resources?

For deeper consideration, read and meditate on Luke 21:1-4 and 2 Corinthians 8:1-7.

By the generosity of your heart, O God, all that we have comes to us by grace freely given, gift-like and unmerited. Strengthen us in the hard work of being honest with ourselves as we practice generosity and serve as stewards of other peoples' gifts. Help us give abundant evidence of your love as we give generously, decide wisely, and lead faithfully.

17
At the Margins

The church fulfills its mission at the margins of the congregation, where those who actively follow Christ encounter those who are not a part of the community of faith. Picture a congregation as concentric circles. In the center circle are the pastor, the leaders and staff, and key volunteers who plan and think and pray and act to lead the church. Farther out is the circle that includes other leaders, including teachers, volunteers, and helpers, and then another circle for those who attend and participate in worship, work projects, and Bible studies. The next larger circle includes all those who attend with less consistency.

When we reach the edge of the farthest circle, we discover on the other side of the margin the people who are not part of the community of faith. The church fulfills its mission at that edge, where those who belong to the community engage and interweave their lives with those outside the community. There, at the margin, we fulfill our mission, through *service and justice* ministries—helping, serving, relieving suffering; and through our *sharing the good* news of Christ—seeking, inviting, welcoming, and nurturing faith. In a missional church, the boundary is wonderfully permeable, and members reach across the edge and new people easily enter into the faith community. The mission of the church is not fulfilled in church planning meetings composed of church members talking with other members about church business, although those meetings may be important to strategize about the mission. The margin is where the action is.

Jesus focused his attention on the margins of the community, usually over the objection of the religious leaders of his day and the counsel of his followers. Nearly every Gospel story involves Jesus speaking with the marginalized: calling tax collectors, healing lepers, engaging a woman at the well, interceding on behalf of a woman accused of adultery, receiving children, challenging money-changers, praying with a thief on the cross. We have no stories of Jesus attending meetings! When he does gather his disciples, he draws their attention to the people at the margins: "just as you did it to one of the least of these who are members of my family . . ." (Matthew 25:40 NRSV).

Leading involves redirecting the attention of the congregation toward the margins where we fulfill the mission of Christ. Leading means outward-focused thinking.

Early Methodist conferences refreshed pastors and laity in their attention to the mission field. The mission was not fulfilled at conference; rather, conference was a means of reinvigorating one another for continued engagement with the mission field.

We could describe the general church with concentric circles as well, with bishops and general agencies and general conference somewhere in the center, then annual conferences and their ministries farther out, and then congregations where the mission is fulfilled.

No offense to bishops or conference staff, but the mission of the church is not fulfilled in conference offices. Conference offices don't feed the homeless, counsel the bereaved, or host divorce recovery groups. Rather, conference leaders *strengthen congregations* to fulfill the mission. In effect, *we help people to help people.* Congregations don't exist to support the conference; the conference exists to start and strengthen congregations and to develop the leadership streams to make that possible. We lead congregations to lead people to active faith in Jesus Christ.

Many general agencies are one more step removed from the locus of the mission than the conference is. The General Board of Discipleship or The United Methodist Publishing House do not teach people the faith; they teach people to teach people. The General Board of Higher Education and Ministry does not lead people to faith, it prepares people to lead people to faith. Other agencies, such as the General Board of Global Ministries, provide channels and connections throughout the world that expand our understanding of the neighbors our congregations are called to serve.

Sometimes we prepare reams of petitions to present at conference sessions or lists of recommended policy changes to our congregations in the belief that if the petitioners can win a majority vote of approval for their cause, we have fulfilled the mission of the church. But the mission of the church is not accomplished at meetings, no matter how large; or by petitions, no matter how well-crafted; or by changes in the budget, no matter how well-motivated. At best, these are preparatory. At worst, they represent avoidance behaviors that keep us focused inwardly on the organization.

Within a mile of your church, an elderly person lives alone, feeling abandoned and isolated. Within a mile of your church, a couple struggles to strengthen the last threads of love that bind them together. Within that radius, children live with no one to invite them to the spiritual life or to the community that can help them discover God's grace. A middle-class family struggles under the anxieties of losing a job, and an immigrant family lives in fear. A teenager contemplates suicide. Within a mile of your church, dozens of people wrestle with personal addictions related to alcohol, prescription drugs, or illegal substances. Hundreds of people carry burdens of unresolved guilt and grief and despair, and do not belong to sustaining communities who surround them with love. Hundreds more wonder about the purpose and meaning of their lives, and do not have the vocabulary to express their inner longings and searching as spiritual hunger.

The people at the margins of our church represent the mission field entrusted to us by God. They are the reason your church exists. Your church is the means of grace God uses to reach them. And by the grace of God, most of our churches are imbued with the vision and resources to engage far beyond one mile, to reach across the community and around the world.

When we redirect the flow of energy and resources toward increasing the number of vital congregations that make disciples for Jesus Christ for the transformation of the world, this is not about institutional survival, but about missional renewal. Leaders are trying to move the focus of a large, complex organization from the center to the margins once again, to draw our attention to the mission field. Local congregations provide the primary arena through which God works to reach those at the margins in the spirit and way of Jesus. That's why it matters that we offer our utmost and highest to the ministry of Christ through healthy and fruitful communities of faith.

What ministries of your congregation reach the people at the margins? What changes of attitude, behavior, and focus cultivate a deeper sense of mission?

What redirection of conference resources, personnel, and energy might increase the number of congregations that reach out? How does your conference prepare and form people for outward-focused ministry?

To delve deeper, read Luke 15:1-7. What does this passage mean for people at the margins?

Help us forget ourselves enough to truly seek and serve others. Shape our worries into prayers and our prayers into practices that serve your purposes. Make us quick to respond to those in distress. May we never be so irritated, apathetic, or discouraged that we give up, but instead find you in serving our sisters and brothers.

18
Ignore, Deny, Avoid, and Blame

Find a comfortable position in a peaceful place. Bring a cup of coffee. Take a deep breath. Breathe in slowly, and then release. I'm about to share bad news. Everyone who loves you before you read this will love you after you are finished. God is with us. We can handle talking about things we'd rather avoid.

Let's look at why we face some hard decisions in the United Methodist Church:

For nearly fifty years, the majority of our churches have seen uninterrupted decline in attendance. We operate using financial models that are intrinsically unsustainable. Membership and attendance fall while expenses at the local, conference, and general church increase. The closing of churches, the move to part-time ministry, and the reduction of costs for hundreds of churches result in ever-increasing cost shifts to the 15% of our churches that are growing. Some conferences face huge pension liabilities, several seminaries face financial hardship and reduced enrollment, and because of our high median age, we will lose large numbers of our most generous donors during the next two decades.

Most of our congregations are not reaching younger generations. The age disparity between the leadership of our congregations and the communities we serve increases each decade.

Mainline churches are perceived by youth culture as irrelevant, conflicted, hypocritical, insensitive, and out of touch.

Our clergy leadership systems for recruiting, educating, training, credentialing, deploying, evaluating, and (when necessary) removing clergy are not serving us well. The default in most conferences is "if you meet the requirements and have done nothing egregious, you will be approved," rather than "you will likely not be approved unless you demonstrate exceptional fruitfulness and promise for ministry." The number of people approved for commissioning and ordination has no relation to the number needed to serve churches. Even among our most gifted clergy who are excellent at maintaining current ministries, few have the ability to actually transition a declining congregation toward growth.

Our organizational structures are not conducive to our ministry. Local churches struggle with complex disciplinary requirements derived from an era when we expected uniformity. Annual conference sessions conduct business with three times as many people present than thirty years ago, even though we have fewer districts, churches, and members. Vertical alignments between general, conference, district, and local church boards, based on 1950s centralized organizational models, restrict creative contextual organizing according to the mission

We lack clarity about our mission. Most of our churches do poorly at connecting with the unchurched in their communities. We wait for people to come to us and to like our worship styles rather than reaching out to engage people. We began as a "go to" church, but we've become a "come to" denomination.

We are resistant to change, suspicious of accountability, averse to metrics, defensive about letting go, and protective of the patterns and models that have brought us to this point. Congregations long for young adults but will not make the changes that would attract them and involve them in new forms of ministry. Pastors resist asking for help from those who are successfully experimenting with outreach models that work. Conference leaders have difficulty truly aligning resources and personnel toward the mission.

Breathe in. Breathe out. Take a sip of coffee. You are still loved. God is still with us.

I don't pretend to have the answers to all the challenges listed above. This is not a *good people* versus *bad people* discussion. I am one of us. Like you, I've inherited, lived with, worked through, cultivated, benefited from, and led the systems we now have.

The tendency of most organizations when they receive bad news is to *ignore, deny, avoid,* and *blame*. We *ignore* the truth by merely continuing to do business as usual, hoping the bad news will go away. We follow the same patterns, hold the same meetings, and pretend that the trends don't affect us. We *deny* when we reassure ourselves that the decline is not really very serious, or that it's temporary. When people get to know us or if we have a change of pastor or if we remodel the sanctuary, everything will be all right. We *avoid* these issues when we argue over trivialities that have nothing to do with our mission and when we focus on things that are important to us personally but which are not essential to our work. *Blame* is my favorite way of turning our attention away from these challenges. We point to someone else as the source of all our problems—it's the fault of the bishops, the pastors, the seminaries, the general boards, the liberals, the conservatives, the old people, or the young people!

Ignore, deny, avoid, and blame: none of these help us move into a future with hope. Instead, these challenges should inspire in us a healthy sense of urgency and a commitment to take responsibility for the part of the mission of Christ entrusted to us.

If everyone who belongs to your congregation–every pastor, leader, teacher, staff member, volunteer–offered the same frequency, quality and effectiveness of invitation to others to explore the spiritual life and enter the body of Christ that you offer, would your congregation be growing or declining? It is not someone else who needs to change. Every one of us needs to own the mission God gives us, and realize that we need to change our own patterns and attitudes and behaviors.

If every congregation fulfilled the mission of the United Methodist Church just as effectively as your congregation does, would your conference be expanding or declining? If every annual conference in the United Methodist Church aligned its resources, personnel and energy toward the mission of the church in the same way that your annual conference does, would our denomination be growing or diminishing? Rather than ignore, deny, avoid, and blame, perhaps we should reflect on what it means to accept responsibility for the mission of Christ humbly and with a note of repentance, and then rededicate our hearts to the hard work of changing ourselves for the purposes of Christ.

Do you feel the challenges listed above are real and valid concerns which need our attention? What other challenges are critical to our future?

How do you personally feed the passion for ministry while also fostering the patience to work through an organization that responds slowly?

What ministries, initiatives, and experiments with new models and practices give you hope?

For deeper reflection, explore Philippians 4:6-9 from *THE MES-SAGE* for new insight into a familiar teaching.

Forgive us for our complacency and inattention to the people you have sent us to serve. Remove from us the internal obstacles that trip us up every time we try to serve you. Open us, Lord, to honest appraisal, to redemptive confession, to a hopeful future, and to new ways of learning and leading in your name.

19
The Most Significant Arena

Methodism began as a way of life. Wesley organized people into societies, classes, and bands in order to provide a disciplined accountability to sustain growth in Christ and growth in service. Early Wesleyans were chided for their "methodical" adherence to practices that included worship, the sacraments, daily prayers, Bible study, classes, giving to the poor, visiting the sick and imprisoned. Every organizational innovation fostered that way of life. Circuits were created as a means of providing the sacraments and for deploying leaders. Class tickets were given and giving records were maintained, not merely to provide an accounting for the aggregate totals, but to hold each person accountable for growth in Christ. Wesley did not establish faith communities so that he could have a conference; he established a conference to support the work of Christ through faith communities.

Throughout the history of Methodism, the primary means by which we have brought people into this way of life has been through faith communities. Congregations offer the invitation and embrace of Christ. They offer worship that connects people to God and that stimulates the change of heart that transforms lives so that people see the world through God's eyes. Congregations provide the means to grow in faith through small groups, Bible studies, support groups, and the care of souls. People cooperate with the Holy Spirit in their own sanctification, growing in grace and in the knowledge and love of God. And fruitful congregations help people discern the calling of God to ministries of service, mission, and justice. They provide avenues for life-changing, sacrificial service that transforms the world. Congregations draw people into the body of Christ, and through congregations God changes the world.

Consider the impact of congregations on your own life. Suppose we could extract from your life all the influences that God has had on you through congregations. Imagine we could pull out of your mind and heart all the thousands of sermons you have heard, the tens of thousands of hymns you have sung, the pastoral prayers and personal devotions that have formed you. Remove from your life all the pastors, friends, colleagues, laypersons, youth leaders, and teachers who have encouraged and embraced you in the faith. Extract from your soul all the work projects, the meetings, the soup kitchens, mission projects, hospital visits and support from others you have experienced. Remove all the volunteer hours, stewardship campaigns, mission fairs, camp experiences, and youth ministries.

If someone removed from your life all the influences congregations have ever had on you, you'd be someone totally different. The congregations you have belonged to have changed and shaped you. Congregations are a primary means by which God reaches into our lives to work on our behalf to create us anew, to claim us as God's own, and to call us to God's service.

It is through congregations that God's Spirit shapes how we understand ourselves, how we relate to our families, how we view community, and how we participate in the world.

Jesus intentionally formed his followers into a community of disciples to fulfill this mission. United Methodist congregations exist today for the same mission for which Jesus gathered his disciples and for which the Holy Spirit unified those who gathered on the day of Pentecost. The United Methodist Church makes disciples of Jesus Christ for the transformation of the world by repeating over and over again what has happened in your life and mine. In small congregations and large, in urban and rural churches, in every place and culture and language, God works through faith communities to change lives.

The *Call to Action* invites the leaders of The United Methodist Church to redirect the flow of attention, energy, and resources to an intense concentration on fostering and sustaining an increase in the number of vital congregations effective in making disciples of Jesus Christ for the transformation of the world. The focus on congregations is not about institutional survival, an obsession on numbers, or a fear of failure. It is about returning to the basics. In the first sentence that immediately follows our mission statement in the *Book of Discipline,* we say, "Local churches provide *the most significant arena* through which disciple-making occurs" (¶120, italics added).

Imagine if we really allowed this priority on Christ's mission through congregations to direct us in our alignment of resources, personnel, and energy in every district, conference, and general agency of the church. Imagine bishops and superintendents and conference staff and lay leaders and pastors viewing Christ's mission through congregations as job one. Imagine if reaching the poor, the vulnerable, the hurting, and the lonely with ministries driven by the grace of God focused our energies. Imagine fostering congregational leadership and spiritual depth and invitational culture and courageous witness in every community of faith. Imagine how God could use our churches all the more to change lives, foster communities in Christ, and relieve suffering if we really behaved as if local churches provide the most significant arena through which we make disciples of Jesus Christ for the transformation of the world. Imagine!

How has God used faith communities to shape your life? How can decisions by annual conference leaders foster life in Christ for more and more people? How well does your conference do with starting new faith communities and encouraging congregations to do so? How actively does your own congregation support such efforts?

For deeper exploration, read Acts 2:37-47 in *THE MESSAGE* as well as in the NRSV for added perspective, and reflect on the practices that formed the earliest faith communities and how these form congregations today.

With you, Lord, we get a fresh start, we're created new. Help us abandon ways that no longer work, and take up practices that bind us to you and to others with purpose and vitality. Help us see the world through your eyes, Lord, and remake us so that people see you in our eyes.

20
Metrics and the Immeasurables of Ministry

Vines, branches, seeds, vineyards, farmers, fig trees, harvests, sowers, soils, weeds, roots. *Fruitfulness* provides a metaphor for many profound aspects of the spiritual life and the Christian journey.

Jesus uses *fruitfulness* to draw our attention to our impact, the consequence of our ministry and of our life in Christ. He describes kingdom fruit, the effect and promise of the reign of God. Fruit refers to what Christ accomplishes through us. Jesus cursed the fig tree that bore no fruit (see Matthew 21; Mark 11) and describes the pruning of fruitless branches (see John 15). *Fruitless* means inconsequential, ineffective, showing no result. Jesus expects our life of faith and our ministries to make a difference. If it's not working, stop doing it.

Jesus says, "My father is glorified by this, that you bear much fruit and become my disciples" (John 15:8). Fruit evidences discipleship; following Jesus and fruitfulness are inextricably linked. Disciples bear fruit.

The writings of John Wesley are replete with references to fruitfulness. "Have they fruit?" was one question he commonly asked pastors, leaders, and churches.

These teachings and our passionate commitment to Christ's ministry stimulate us to evaluate the impact of our personal ministries, and the ministries of our congregations, conferences, committees, and councils. Honestly, churches, conferences, and other non-profit organizations are usually weak on evaluating outcomes, results, and impacts. The *Call to Action* explicitly invites greater use of metrics and evaluation to measure outcomes at all levels of the church. Some people celebrate this as a positive step, and others see this as acquiescence to corporate organizational models that have nothing to do with the spiritual life. But doesn't Jesus clearly emphasize fruitfulness?

The fruit of some ministries are easily measured—in numbers of people participating, real changes in life conditions, homes rebuilt, dollars given, meals served, inequities resolved, illnesses cured. Other fruit seem beyond measure—the changes of the human heart, the growth in compassion, the stirrings of the call to service. Just because some aspects of ministry are immeasurable does not free us of the God-given call to focus on fruitfulness.

When we become unclear about our mission and fail to focus on fruitful outcomes, we begin to measure "inputs" instead of fruit, taking great satisfaction in how many people, meetings, dollars, buildings, and hours we've given to a task with little regard to whether these things have truly changed lives or made any real difference. Many churches and conferences have come to believe that spending more money, having a larger staff, holding more meetings, and preparing longer reports are progress. But these are all inputs. They are not fruit. The purpose of the church is the changed life—hearts deepened in Christ, children protected from malaria, vulnerable people sustained against injustice, the poor receiving access to education, mourners supported by the grace of community. There are thousands of ways of impacting lives through the ministry of Christ and a thousand forms of fruitful ministry. Some are measurable, and these we should count and learn how to do better. Where we cannot measure outcomes, we can describe changes and bear witness to the visible signs of the Spirit's invisible work through us and our churches.

I readily confess that there are limits and problems with metrics, including finding the right things to measure that reflect and enhance ministry for churches, conferences, boards, and councils. Many strategies have us counting membership in a time when people are not joining, worship attendance in an era when people relate to the church in countless ways beyond worship, baptisms when parents are allowing their children to decide for themselves at a later age, and Sunday school attendance when most small-group discipleship takes place during the week. And far too many pastors, local church leaders, and cabinets are using numbers with an implicit "contingent/reward" modality: if I do *this,* then I earn, deserve, or receive *that.* This use of metrics risks becoming a disincentive to creative ministry.

However, when metrics are used properly, they become tools toward an end and toward the goal of changed lives. They help us understand what works and what doesn't, and how to redirect resources toward greater fruitfulness. Even if we measure imperfectly and even though much of ministry is immeasurable, we have an obligation to focus on fruitfulness. Otherwise, we simply increase budgets, staffs, buildings, and meetings in ways that are unintentionally but insidiously self-serving, institutional, and in-ward-focused.

When Jesus says, "I am the vine; you are the branches," he reminds us that all our fruits derive from our relationship to God in Christ. When Jesus says, "and they will know them by their fruit," this should make us extraordinarily attentive to the end and purpose of our calling. Our fruit is God's fruit.

What do you see as the fruit of your personal ministry as a layperson or pastor? How does God use you to shape the lives of people around you and through them to change the world?

What are the most fruitful ministries of your congregation? What are the least fruitful? Of your conference? Do ministries need to be pruned? Do new seeds need to be planted?

How do you deal with the fact that some outcomes are clearly measurable and some are not? What fruits are describable even when they are not easily measurable?

How does the discipline of focusing on fruitfulness strengthen ministry? How does an attentiveness to fruitfulness shape your discussions, deliberations, and decisions as a church leader?

For deeper consideration, read John 15:1-17 or search the New Testament using a concordance or online resource for the words *fruit* or *fruits.*

Help us put defensiveness, self-deception, and fear aside, Lord, to look at the fruitfulness of our work through your eyes. Strengthen and bless our congregation so that we may discover your presence anew and change the lives of people you call us to serve. Use us, Lord, for you.

21
The Big Rocks

A story in *First Things First* describes a lesson about the use of time.[1] The instructor fills a large jar with big rocks until he cannot possibly add another rock. He asks the audience if the jar is full. Everyone agrees that there is no more room for more rocks. Then he lifts a container of pebbles, and pours them into the same jar. The pebbles tumble loosely between the spaces left by the rocks, settling into place. Again, he asks if the jar is full. People are now wise to his ploy and are less willing to agree. Next, he lifts a container of sand and pours it into the jar, and people watch as the sand cascades through all the loose spaces between the rocks and pebbles. "Now, is the jar full?" The audience agrees that the jar is completely filled and has no room for anything else. Then he pours a glass of water into the jar, and the water trickles from top to bottom, saturating the sand and pebbles and rocks.

"What have we learned about the use of time?" he asks. Someone says, "You can always squeeze one more thing into an already crowded schedule!" "No," the instructor answers, "we've learned that *if we don't place the big rocks in first, we can never squeeze them in later.*" The story is about priority.[2]

Keeping the main thing the main thing requires intentionality.

What's the one activity or practice of yours that done consistently (and consistently well!) would have the greatest positive impact on your ministry as a lay person or as a pastor?

When I was working on the book *Five Practices of Fruitful Congregations,* I would stop by a coffee shop each morning to write for about an hour. One day as I was writing, I couldn't help but overhear a conversation in the booth next to me. A mother and her teenage daughter sat on one side of the table while another mother and daughter sat on the other side. The first mother was asking about how the other family had heard about their church and whether they'd been part of a church before. Then she quietly told how her own family had come to the church and about what the congregation meant for them. Her daughter chimed in telling about cool and exciting things the youth did together. The conversation was easy-going, informative, exploratory, and done in a loving way. The first mother then took a few minutes to talk about the youth ministry of the church and to answer questions. I had witnessed a sacred moment of invitation and hospitality.

The next day I sat at the same table in the same coffee shop to do my writing. In the nearby booth, a father and his teenage son sat on one side of the table and another father and son sat on their other side. I overheard nearly the same conversation as I had witnessed the day before! Suddenly I realized what was going on. In this congregation, whenever a young person visited the youth ministry, one of the parents who already belonged to the church would invite the visitors for coffee in order to connect with them, to learn about them, to welcome them to the church, and to answer any questions that would ease their entry into the community of faith.   Compare this system for welcoming visitors to that of our own youth ministries. I would be delighted if visiting families to our churches at least received a post card or phone call. This practice goes the second mile. This congregation doesn't settle for mediocrity. These folks engage on a personal and deeply meaningful level. Obviously, the congregation considers reaching young people and welcoming visitors to be among the Big Rocks that must come first.

I wrote *Five Practices of Fruitful Congregations* to answer the question, "What are the most important things for congregations to focus our work on to fulfill the mission of Christ?" Church councils spend inordinate amounts of time debating facilities, budgets, schedules, and planning more meetings. These are important, but we dare not focus on them to the exclusion of what is essential. If we do not repeat, deepen, and improve upon the basic fundamental practices of ministry—Radical Hospitality, Passionate Worship, Intentional Faith Development, Risk-Taking Mission and Service, and Extravagant Generosity—then our mission weakens a little more each year. The Five Practices are the fundamental activities that are so critical to the mission of the church that failure to perform them in an exemplary way leads to diminishing ministry. They are the Big Rocks of congregational ministry.

Or, what are the one or two activities that are so critical to the mission of your conference that they must be done consistently with excellence in order to extend the ministry of Christ through congregations? Our conference has answered with Congregational Excellence and Pastoral Excellence. Congregational Excellence means we focus on starting new congregations, exploring alternative forms of faith communities for college-age adults, and strengthening existing congregations. Pastoral Excellence involves systems for recruiting, developing, educating, training, supporting, and evaluating gifted clergy who are spiritually grounded, emotionally healthy, effective and fruitful leaders. If we fail at these tasks, or fail to do them with excellence, there will be no conference in the future. These are the Big Rocks of conference ministry.

Churches and conferences are complex organizations with multiple moving parts. Budgets, meetings, facilities, staff, salaries, insurance, and hundreds of other important things fill our agendas, dominate our conversations, and consume our time. But if we don't place the Big Rocks in first, we have trouble squeezing them in later.

What are the activities that are so critical to your congregation's mission that failure to perform them with excellence leads to decline? What about your conference's mission?

For engaging Scripture, think about the word *first* in the stories of Jesus: *"first* be reconciled to your brother" . . . "strive *first* for the kingdom of God" . . . *"first* take the log out of your own eye" . . . *"first* let me go and bury my father" . . . *"first* sit down and estimate the cost" . . . "the greatest and *first* commandment" . . .

"whoever wishes to be *first* among you" (Matthew 5:24; 6:33; 7:5; 8:21; Luke 14:28; Matthew 22:38; Matthew 20:27 or Mark 10:44 NRSV). What do we learn about priorities for our life and ministry from these references?

Dear God, help us distinguish between what is merely convenient, easy, and rewarding for us and what is essential for serving others with real love and respect. Help us grab the initiative to treat others as we would want to be treated.

22
Logjam

I run along a bike trail that has a number of small bridges stretched across creeks and streams. These former railway structures were built with thick steel girders that rise high above the creek beds. I often pause in the middle of a bridge to look down for fish, snakes, or turtles, and to listen to the refreshing gurgles of the stream through the rocks.

After a few days of hard rain upstream, the soothing picture changes. The small streams become raging currents that rise to the bottom of the bridge. During flood conditions, the steel girders form a grate that catches tons of sticks, branches, and logs until the combined effect is a dangerously large and impenetrable dam of densely-pressed debris. I can feel the bridge shudder under the pressure of the flow against the blockage. As I look at the tons of accumulated matter, I wonder, "Where did all this come from? What happens if all these branches and logs and trunks totally dam up the streaming flow?"

I've just described a logjam. Any one branch or stick or log does no damage and has no effect on the flow. But if the stream picks up enough of them, and they seize together at a narrow spot, then the results can lead to disaster—the stream is stopped, the floodwaters overflow the banks, or the bridge is put at risk.

Logjams are risks to organizations as well. Remember, my friends, that I am one of us, and I've poured my life into the task of serving the church I love. I do not offer critical observations in order to feed cynicism or anti-denominational feeling. But as I've watched the effect of successive General Conferences and Annual Conferences and Church Conferences, I've often felt that many of the changes we make to policy and practice result in tossing more logs and sticks and branches into the stream, a practice that inevitably contributes to the formation of logjams for our mission.

Each individual change may grow from positive motive, but the cumulative effect can be dangerous to our mission. I'm not arguing for or against any particular requirement; it is the combined effect that limits the flow of creativity and adaptability and responsiveness. If you wish to see what I mean, look at the United Methodist *Book of Discipline* paragraphs related to the Conference Board of Higher Education and Campus Ministry (¶634) and you will see nearly sixty duties and responsibilities. Look at the list of more than thirty "Specific Responsibilities of District Superintendents" (¶419–425) or check out the fifteen other places in the *Discipline* that speak of Superintendent responsibilities. Annual Conferences often have nearly as many regulations in their Standing Rules, and even congregations easily go overboard with zillions of explicit policies or implicit protocols that limit and restrict how people perform their ministries. If new committee members sit down to study their tasks, the list of accumulated requirements would more than occupy the whole calendar year before they even consider their own context, mission fields, or their own gifts and callings.

All the policies and rules were adopted because well-meaning individuals, committees, constituencies, and boards offered ideas to address concerns, redress problems, and increase ministry by prescribing church-wide remedies. But the effect is as if each of us picked up a branch and set it afloat in the stream. We've unknowingly contributed to the logjam, the experience of intransigence and paralysis that we see at nearly every level of the church, of people focused and absorbed by unending and unclear policies, procedures, and requirements to the neglect of the mission field around them.

Logjam describes the inevitable intertwining and accumulation of policies, procedures, standards, requirements, and structures that result from years of recorded decisions in a mature organization. The dense, impenetrable mass stifles creativity, blocks the flow of innovation, discourages experimentation, and thwarts inventiveness.

Methodism began as a *movement*. Life and faith are fluid and flowing. Growth involves adaptation, change, creativity, motion. The principal identifying elements of our tradition began as tools to maximize adaptability and movement—itinerancy, connectionalism, conference, and episcopacy. These were strategies to enhance maximum flexibility and responsiveness to changing circumstances and opportunities.

Recently someone asked me if organizational changes at General Conference or at Annual Conferences can really make any difference in whether we have more vital congregations. In the short term, growing churches will continue to grow and declining churches will continue to decline no matter what General Conference does. But in the long term, it matters how we address issues of clergy recruitment, education, training, deployment, and evaluation. It matters how we realign resources to start new congregations, develop ways to interrupt decline, and help congregations focus on their mission fields. It matters that our leaders focus on the right questions and deal with issues relevant to our mission around the globe. It matters that we connect our money to our mission. It matters that we leave a legacy to the next generation, not of complex and impenetrable rules and ineffective systems, but of a church that is clear about its mission and confident about its future, and which is agile and responsive and engaged with the world for the purposes of Christ.

Can you think of "logjam" policies and procedures that limit creative response in your congregation? In your conference?

How do we avoid innocently contributing to organizational intransigence? As a leader, how do you help sustain the life of the Spirit and of community in Christ as something alive, fluid, and flowing?

For deeper consideration, read some of the passages in which Jesus confronts the corrupting influence of systems more tied to their rules than to their God-given purposes. For a fresh look at Matthew 23, read it in Peterson's translation, *THE MESSAGE.* Or if that's too harsh, read Luke 6:1-11.

Lord, untangle us, and free us for joyful, passionate obedience to your callings. Help us ever see the larger picture of the life you show us in Christ and of the kingdom you seek to advance in the world.

23
The Vicious Habit

Elections are drawing near in the US, and I'm already feeling bombarded by political ads. They barge into my driving time through radio spots, interrupt the rare moments I enjoy watching television, arrive uninvited to my email address, and fill my mailbox with leaflets. I'm disappointed and embarrassed by the viciousness and distortion from both parties. The tactics seem cheap, harmful, and empty of any attempt at honest, thorough, and serious engagement with the issues we face. Many ads feature grainy, black-and-white photos of an opponent taken from an unflattering angle to contrast with the polished, wholesome, color pictures of the candidate being supported. Extreme and negative hyperbole distorts motives of opponents and attacks their ideas without presenting meaningful, positive alternative proposals. It's hard to find meaningful dialogue.

Criticizing political ads is convenient and popular. It's easy to blame politicians, their strategists, and the media. Why have ads become so vicious and distorted? Evidently, negative ads work. Those who receive these ads are willing to avoid the hard work of learning about complex issues. We are happy to nod our heads based on 30-second soundbites rather than delve deeper and to think beyond our self-interest to the good of the nation and world. We're willing to be seduced and deceived by oversimplification.

The same tendencies can shape our church life, including a propensity to oversimplify ideas, vilify opponents, and protect our own prerogatives.

"Most people, given the choice between having a better world, or a better place within the world as it is, would choose the latter." We might restate this observation, attributed to 20th-century Methodist preacher, Ralph Sockman, for church leadership: Most people, given the choice between having a better conference, or a better place within the conference as it is, would choose the latter." We can even change *conference* to *congregation!*

I don't think people always pursue their own self-interest above the good of the whole organization. In a more nuanced way, we vote based on behaviors and assumptions with which we are familiar, find comfortable, and want to hold onto without carefully testing whether the behaviors we defend are best in the current context or whether the assumptions are still valid for the mission of the church today. We have trouble letting go

One can discern a rhythm in church conferences and annual conferences. Those present move from moments of profound communion to times when they feel palpable mistrust. On the one hand, we use organic models for community to describe and celebrate our relationship with one another—body of Christ, members, communion, bread, family, sisters, brothers. Our singing and praying and preaching unify us in Christ. On the other hand, we use adversarial strategies for deciding business, experiencing conference as a cauldron of competing self-interests and personal agendas. Rather than a gathering to listen, learn, discern, and decide together on goals for the church, our conferring together seems a collection of people seeking to win advantage in their effort to represent an idea, protect a project, or pursue an agenda with little regard for competing claims. Some groups depend upon the cohesive quality of fear to mobilize response. Church leaders find it difficult to moderate conflict when they are motivated to win at any cost.

This places upon leaders a great responsibility to foster the unifying elements of our life together in Christ. With leadership in the church comes immense responsibility. And the person with the fullest cup requires the steadiest hands.

An organization marked by intense disagreements that aspires to communion requires intentionality in how the members pursue passions with humility and accept limits to their will with grace. Can a diverse body of people have a process that is fair, prayerful, and civil, and yet focuses on the mission of the church? Can conferences and congregations foster such an atmosphere when it means some desires of nearly every member go unfulfilled?

Paul writes about the need to moderate divisive or self-serving motives while remaining passionate for the purposes of Christ. He reminds us to be ardent in spirit, to hold fast, and to seek what is good and acceptable and perfect. On the other hand, he instructs us to love one another with mutual affection, to let love be genuine, to live in harmony, and to not think more highly of ourselves than we ought to think (see Romans 12). Balance passion and courage with humility and confession. We are one body in Christ, members of one another, and yet we have gifts and perspectives that differ. None of us sees the whole truth.

Paul was not inviting us to deny hard realities; rather, he was asking us to deal with hard realities with integrity, faithfulness, and graciousness. There's nothing distinctly Christian about being gracious; but if we are distinctly Christian, then graciousness, truth, and fairness characterize our interests, involvements, and behaviors. In another place, Paul writes:

> It is obvious what kind of life develops out of trying to get your own way all the time: repetitive, loveless . . . cut-throat competition; all-consuming-yet-never-satisfied wants; a brutal temper; an impotence to love or be loved; divided homes and divided lives; small-minded and lop-sided pursuits; the vicious habit of depersonalizing every-one into a rival; . . . ugly parodies of community. . . .If you use your freedom this way, you will not inherit God's kingdom. . . .But what happens when we live God's way? He brings gifts into our lives, much the same way that fruit appears in an orchard—things like affection for oth-ers, exuberance about life, serenity. We develop a willing-ness to stick with things, a sense of compassion in the heart, and a conviction that a basic holiness permeates things and people. We find ourselves involved in loyal commitments, not needing to force our way in life, able to marshal and direct our energies wisely."
>
> Galatians 5:19–22 *THE MESSAGE*

The phrase that jumps out is "the vicious habit of deperson-alizing everyone into a rival." In Christ, we can do better. None of us has ever belonged to any organization or community where we have not at some point disagreed with others or with the decision of the majority. The unity of the church is a hard and unending task entrusted to all who follow Christ. More than a political strategy, this is a spiritual necessity, a calling of God through Christ. Thinking alike is not mandatory, but living as one in the body of Christ is essential.

How do you remain passionately engaged with those who view things differently from you in your own congregation? At conference?

In your spiritual life, how do you balance the ardent spirit that propels you to action with a sense of humility and community?

To move deeper, meditate on Romans 12:1-2.

Focus our hearts on things true, noble, authentic, compelling, and gracious—the best, not the worst; the life-giving rather than the life-sapping. Build us up in you, Lord. Thank you for deep-spirited friends and for all those people you send into our lives to share our journeys in you.

24
A Culture of Learning

Ronald Heifetz, in *Leadership on the Line,* makes a helpful distinction between adaptive challenges and technical challenges. When a congregation faces a *technical challenge,* we know what the problem is and we know what the solution is, and so our work is to apply the solution to the problem. With an *adaptive challenge,* we don't know what the problem is and we don't know what the solution is, and so congregational leaders must learn new things to identify the underlying issues and to explore possible steps forward.

For instance, suppose the church roof leaks during rainstorms. Everyone knows what the problem is, and that the solution involves replacing the roof. A roofer can be consulted who has the expertise to solve the problem, and when the problem is solved, the situation is restored to how it was before the leak began. Church leaders have to decide how to pay for the work, and they may debate which roofing company to employ, but both the problem and the solution are easily identified and widely understood. A leaking roof is a technical challenge.

Contrast the leaking roof to this challenge: we have no young people in our church anymore. What is the problem? Why are there no children or young adults? Is the problem the pastor? Or the location of the church? Or the changing demographics of the neighborhood? Or the old facility? Or the worship style? Or the music? Or the friendliness of the congregation? Or the perceptions of youth culture toward religion? Or the attitude of the congregation toward noisy children? Or the priorities that drive the budget?

The decrease in young people likely results from a combination of factors, and the pastor, the leaders, and the congregation have to do considerable learning merely to identify and understand what the problem is, and then they have to do considerable learning, exploration, and experimentation in order to discover solutions.

A decrease in young people is an adaptive challenge rather than a technical one. There's no obvious single cause and no easy solution that an expert can offer. Rather than applying a known solution to a known problem, the whole church may have to adapt its behaviors, attitudes, and values in order to move toward a solution. What behaviors shut newcomers out, or make the church unappealing to younger generations, or make parents with young children uncomfortable? Do current members value their own preferences and conveniences more highly than cultivating the faith expressions of young adults? Are we willing to learn and adapt in order to achieve a different future?

Heifetz suggests that the most common mistake an organization makes is treating adaptive challenges as if they were technical challenges. We think the answers are easy, and don't require us to change. How do we deal with the problem of missing young people? Since we replaced the roof and that stopped the leak, let's replace the pastor and that will fix our problems with reaching young people! Adaptive challenges are not that easy. Merely changing one or two factors will likely make little difference. The issues run much deeper.

The role of leadership, according to Heifitz, is to mobilize people to meet the adaptive challenges that are essential for the mission. Organizations tend to avoid, deny, or ignore their adaptive challenges. But pastors and congregational leaders must focus sustained attention on the challenge, and help the whole organization initiate the learning and discovery and exploration that is necessary to move forward toward solutions. Leaders move people through the changes of behavior, attitude, and value that take us toward a more hopeful future.

The *Call to Action* identifies the adaptive challenge for the United Methodist Church as the task of increasing the number of vital congregations that make disciples of Jesus Christ for the transformation of the world. This changes how bishops, cabinets, general boards, annual conferences, and congregations do their work. Adaptive challenges cause everyone to rethink their own values, attitudes, and behaviors. What would have to change about you and me and how we learn and lead in order for us to reverse decline, increase our outreach, and strengthen our congregations?

Fruitful congregations share a common characteristic. They cultivate a culture of learning among the leaders, pastors, and volunteers. When they encounter an obstacle, problem, or restraint in their ministry, they move into an intense learning mode. Suppose a congregation faces a staffing problem, an issue with their music ministry, or a stumbling block with their youth program. The pastor and leaders search the internet to learn from other churches that face similar issues. They call other pastors and leaders to ask questions. They read books on the topic. They load up the church van and take people to a workshop that addresses the issue, or they visit another church to observe their effective ministries. They invite leaders from other churches to evaluate their situation or they contract with a consultant. They read, talk, visit, process, analyze, and learn their way through to new approaches. They overcome the obstacle, and move on until they encounter another challenge, and then the process begins again. They lead through continuous cycles of learning.

In contrast, many congregations hit a snag and they do not deal with it. Unaddressed and unresolved, the problem becomes a limiting factor to their ministry. The congregation moves along until they encounter another issue, avoid dealing with it, and so restrain their ministry yet again. The ministry becomes narrower and weaker because leaders have never addressed the tough challenges, only surrendered to the obstacles. Both the pastor and the lay leadership have to continuously learn so that they can identify and understand the issues that challenge us, and then they must learn in order to formulate next steps and to move forward toward a future with hope.

Searching the web, calling other pastors and leaders, books, workshops, visits to other churches, visits from other church leaders, consultants. . . . How does your congregation learn? How do you learn to lead?

Name one or two adaptive challenges you think your congregation now faces. Name one for your conference. What are the first steps to begin to understand the real problems?

Read Matthew 5: 38-48, thinking about the change of values, attitudes, and behaviors Jesus stimulates in his disciples.

Change is hard for us, Lord. And yet yours is a Spirit that moves through us and around us where it will. You never let us sit still for long. Move us now to new ways of thinking and serving. Open our hearts and minds to honest assessment and courageous commitments.

25

While It Was Still Dark

Can congregations change? Can God breathe new life into congregations as surely as God's grace can interrupt and redirect a person's journey? Can congregations with a long pattern of numerical decline, of decreasing financial support and rising maintenance costs, of fewer new people and an increasing median age renew its purpose, reverse the trends, and grow? Can cultural values, deeply imbedded attitudes, and long-standing patterns of behavior shift so radically that leaders begin to think and practice differently in order to reach the changing community around them and the next generation?

In Oakton, Missouri (population 24), a United Methodist open-country congregation declined for forty years until only 60 people were left. However, during the last 12 years the church has grown to nearly 500 in worship, moved into a new facility, and has 150 children attending Sunday school. A licensed local pastor led the turn-around until his retirement, and now his son, another licensed local pastor, has led the congregation to start a Hispanic congregation that already has nearly 100 people attending. The church offers recovery ministries locally while globally, the congregation generously supports UMCOR and Child Rescue in the Sierra Leone Conference. Oakton United Methodist Church provides a positive witness that draws people from miles away in a county whose population is declining.

First UMC of Sikeston, Missouri, watched its attendance decline for nearly 50 years, even under the leadership of excellent pastors, until it settled into an average of 320. Congregational leaders courageously invited a Healthy Church Initiative consultation, and accepted recommendations regarding outreach, facility, staffing, and worship. They used coaches and consultants and mystery visitors. They prayed and learned and worked. They initiated community service projects, and then reached to other parts of the state and world with life-changing ministries. During the last two years, the congregation's attendance has increased by nearly 150 people, and more young people are involved. *Outreach Magazine* named First UMC, Sikeston, the fastest growing mid-sized congregation in the US.

Last year in Kansas City, a young African-American clergy-woman started Renaissance, a multicultural congregation with 140 people each week, in a facility that previously belonged to a church that had dwindled to 12 members. The new church bustles with young people in one of the three poorest school districts in the state. Also, in downtown Kansas City, the Missouri Conference cooperated with a congregation from another conference to start Church of the Resurrection Downtown. They've converted a bar into a place of worship, with 600 people attending weekly, mostly young adults who have had no previous faith affiliation.

In Sedalia, Missouri, First UMC risked a second site and built a wonderfully inviting, child-friendly facility while also continuing worship in their historic downtown facility. Attendance that had declined for decades has grown in the last 15 years from 130 to nearly 900, with 2,500 people attending recent Easter services!

In urban St. Louis, in a story reminiscent of Elijah passing the mantle of ministry to the next generation, Immanuel UMC, which had declined to a handful of elderly members, closed its doors. The facility was given to a new church called The Gathering of St. Louis. The Gathering renovated the building, reached out to mostly young professionals, with worship that combines weekly Communion with excellent contemporary music. The congregation averages 600 people after five years, raised more than $100,000 last Christmas Eve for the Mozambique Safe Water Project and to deepen their partnership with Kingdom House, a UM community center, and has started a second site in another facility where a church has closed. The second site already averages 160 people.

In the suburban rim surrounding Kansas City, most of the United Methodist congregational growth has resulted from relocations of long-time churches that have followed the population. With new facilities adapted to the lifestyles of their communities, they are thriving. Lee's Summit UMC averages an attendance of 1,400 today compared to 620 a dozen years ago, and Woods Chapel has an attendance of 1,200 today, up from 600. Woods Chapel provides one of the most extensive disaster-relief ministries in the state, and has maintained teams in Joplin without interruption since tornados struck nearly one year ago.

In rural Calhoun, Missouri, a licensed lay minister accepted an assignment to serve a congregation of fewer than 20 people. For four years, she has led the congregation through extraordinary growth, numerous building improvements, and an ever-expanding ministry to the community. Attendance now averages more than 40.

These United Methodist congregations are samples of a significant number of churches that have figured out how to reverse decline, strengthen ministry, broaden outreach, and move toward greater fruitfulness. They fulfill their missions in areas of population decline as well as growth: in rural, urban, and suburban settings, and with small, medium, and larger memberships. Decline is not inevitable. Resurgence of spirit and vision can happen. God can breathe new life into congregations.

Every US conference has congregations that buck the trends. The purpose behind the *Call to Action* is to cultivate a systemic organizational environment in our conferences and general church that fosters new life, new learning, and new missional outreach in more and more congregations so that we can more fruitfully and faithfully fulfill the mission God gives us in Christ.

Sometimes our emphasis on the joy of resurrection fosters the illusion that new life in Christ is disconnected from and unrelated to death. This is untrue in our personal discipleship—dying to self is part of rebirth and new life. "For those who want to save their life will lose it, and those who lose their life for my sake will save it" (Luke 9:24). And when we speak of the body of Christ, the church, we also discover that new life is found in pouring ourselves out, in dying to old ways, in embracing a new path in Christ.

In John 20 (NRSV), the story of the resurrection of Christ begins with the words "while it was still dark. . . ." The most momentous event in faith history happened while nearly everyone was asleep. It was discovered by grieving followers before the light of dawn. They had no idea that the days to come would be forever different from anything they had yet experienced. God had plans for them they could not possibly imagine. The same is true for us.

The resurrection of Christ renders permanent all that was revealed about God in Jesus' earthly life—that God loves us with an everlasting love, that God's grace extends to all, that God invites us to follow and calls us to serve and sustains us in ministry and sends us forth to share God's way. And we discover in the resurrection of Christ the truth that life defeats death and hope breaks through despair.

What are the signs of new life in your discipleship? What are signs of new life in your congregation? Your conference?

What attitudes, behaviors, and values need to die in order for your congregation to focus on the mission of Christ? Do you believe congregations can really change?

To delve deeper, read John 20:1-18.

Help us in our common work for you "to sing a new song to the Lord," to be created and re-created again and again by your Holy Spirit for the task of sharing the good news that God has met our highest hopes and deepest needs in Jesus Christ. Bless us to your purposes.

26
"Laid Aside by Thee"

The Covenant Prayer, composed and adapted by John Wesley, invites complete humility and obedience to God's service, asking God to work through us or to work around us, and to take us to places and to put us alongside people we would never choose if left to our own inclinations.

> I am no longer my own, but thine.
> Put me to what thou wilt, rank me with whom thou wilt.
> Put me to doing, put me to suffering.
> Let me be employed by thee or laid aside by thee,
>   exalted for thee or brought low by thee.
> Let me be full, let me be empty.
> Let me have all things, let me have nothing.
> I freely and heartily yield all things
>   to thy pleasure and disposal.[1]

Like many United Methodist leaders, I have prayed Wesley's Covenant prayer hundreds of times, sometimes in gatherings and many times quietly on my own. The prayer always has the power to unsettle me and provoke me to deeper reflection about my own motives. Repeating the prayer strengthens me while also making me more attentive to my spiritual vulnerabilities. It restrains my propensity to use the language of God's will to describe and defend what is merely most convenient and desirable for me. It curbs my natural tendency to justify my own views and desired outcomes and forces me to wrestle with what submission to God in Christ truly means for my ministry. Several phrases penetrate the veneers I hide behind to preserve my pride and ambition. It's a powerful prayer, but be careful where it leads you!

The line that disturbs me the most is, "let me be employed by thee, or laid aside by thee." This forces me to face the truth that while God works *through* me to achieve certain good things in the world, God also works *around* me to achieve many other good things. Sometimes I'm not the right person. Sometimes I don't have the right gifts, the right strategies, the right voice, or the right ideas for this particular moment and context of ministry. My ways, my experiences, my passions, my certitudes and biases and approaches may not be the ones for this particular time and for a particular work God needs accomplished.

Sometimes my conference, my staff, my congregation, my friends, my seminary, my board, or my committee is the one that is ripe and ready for the task, and other times mine is the one that must be set aside so that God's good purpose can be fulfilled in another way by someone else. There are challenges that are not mine to resolve and strategies that are not mine to develop. The institutions where I have found my place and the methods I have developed are sometimes those that need to be set aside because the season for which they served is past or because another voice and another approach are needed to reach a generation I cannot.

During a period of complex change in our culture, leaders of Christ's church—lay and clergy—face many hard decisions that require our utmost discernment and highest commitment. Sometimes we must make decisions that do not continue the systems of leadership we have grown accustomed to. Those of us who are most at home with the existing activities and arrangements are likely to most keenly experience the impact of such changes as personal setbacks. Even those who know that change is necessary will consider such suggestions strategic mistakes and ill-advised tampering. They will feel the losses far more acutely than they will see the opportunities. Most of the people in congregational and conference leadership today, including laity, pastors, and bishops, have been the beneficiaries of the systems that have brought us to this point, and so they naturally grieve the losses that come with transitions. And yet the models, behaviors, and attitudes that we need to let go of are the models, behaviors, and attitudes that got us this far. This requires a spiritual maturity that surpasses mere organizational strategy.

How do I pray for the fulfillment of God's purposes when sometimes fulfilling them leaves me on the sidelines or redirects my path from what I had expected? How do I develop the humility to be laid aside graciously, and even joyfully? God has work for me to do as long as I have breath, but sometimes it is not the work I expected. Praying deeply the Covenant Prayer requires discernment, a countercultural spirituality and a counterintuitive openness to God. It requires saying with Jesus that we have come "not to be served but to serve" (Mark 10:45 NRSV). It requires accepting the emotional impact of truly believing that "those who find their life will lose it, and those who lose their life for my sake will find it" (Matthew 10:39 NRSV). It prompts us to think about what it means to no longer be our own, but God's, and causes us to meditate on what it means to yield and step aside with humility.

When was a time you experienced God working around you rather than through you? How did it feel? How did you handle any negative feelings of uselessness or abandonment, and how did you find a renewed sense of purpose in serving in other ways?

Have you ever voluntarily stepped down or stepped back or stepped aside so that a ministry could move in new directions? Where did the spiritual discernment come from to help you do this?

For deeper consideration, meditate on Matthew 20:20-28.

Dear God, whether we lead or follow, stand or sit, move forward or step back, lift our hands or let others speak, help us to serve you without insisting on our own way. Help us distinguish what is merely convenient, easy, and familiar for us and what is essential for serving others with real love and respect.

27
We See a New Church

I recently spoke with some of the laity, clergy, and bishops who have given direction to the *Call to Action*. Often I return from meetings with a low-grade depression, the discussions confirming the intransigence of the church and the hopelessness of reversing the downward trends that challenge our mission. Not so with this meeting!

As I listened to some of our most creative leaders, I felt a more profound hope than I have in a long time. There's a growing consensus of vision and future that I find compelling.

We see a new church, a church that is clear about its mission and confident about its future, a church that is relevant, reaching out, inviting, alive, agile, and resilient. We see a church that is hopeful, passionate, nimble, called of God, outward-focused, courageous.

Where do we see this new church? It is not yet, and it is not everywhere; nevertheless, there are a thousand signs of its emerging.

We see signs of this new church in those congregations that are thriving, those pockets of excellence that have managed to buck the trends to reach younger generations, to extend the ministry of Christ into unexpected places.

During recent months I've preached in rural congregations led by local pastors and lay ministers that have doubled in attendance, started outreach ministries that change lives, and welcomed new people even from areas with declining population. I've celebrated the merger of urban churches in creative ways we wouldn't have thought possible five years ago, combining the excellent and passionate work of growing congregations with strategic facilities to reach neighborhoods afresh. I've shouted with joy at the success of new congregational starts in African American and Hispanic neighborhoods. I've been humbled by the courage and vision of several long-established congregations who have opened themselves to deep and risky transformation. Many congregations are reappraising their mission, making hard choices, and realigning their resources toward more vigorous, fruitful, outward-focused ministry. I'm moved by the number of pastors who voluntarily join continual learning communities, delving more deeply into the dynamics of congregations and the theology of mission, and learn skills to reach new people.

Are these changes affecting every congregation? No. And yet every conference has congregations that are thriving, pastors willing to teach others, and laypersons with the passion to learn, change, and initiate ministry. We see a new church, with signs evident in church starts, unexpected mergers, experiments with second sites, transformed congregations, gifted young people entering ministry, creative initiatives, and risk-taking outreach.

And we see a new church shaping annual conferences, a serious refocusing after decades of restructuring committees and reshuffling staff. Through much experimentation, several annual conferences have truly realigned resources toward their mission. They lead congregations to lead people to active faith in Jesus Christ because they know that congregations do not exist to serve conferences, but conferences exist to cultivate ministries in congregations and communities. Many conferences take excellence, fruitfulness, and accountability seriously in bold new ways. They radically streamline operations, reevaluate the role of superintendents, focus the appointment system on the mission field, and rethink standards for ministry with attention to fruitfulness. I'm profoundly hopeful when I see conferences redirect the flow of energy, attention, and resources toward increasing the number of fruitful congregations. We can learn from them.

And we see a new church emerging at the general church. Several general agencies are streamlining their operations and reassessing their work. Ideas abound about merging, consolidating, cooperating, removing redundancies, reducing costs, and most important, focusing on the mission of Christ particularly through congregations. Conversations taking place now would not have been possible a few years ago. Suggestions about a governance structure that focuses outwardly on the mission, forces future-oriented thinking, reconnects the local church to the general ministries, and increases accountability—these plans give me hope.

And there is a new spirit in the Council of Bishops. The unanimous adoption of the *Call to Action* with its sustained focus on congregational vitality, the willingness of the Council to confront some of the internal issues that have hampered it, the openness to evaluation, and the development of learning communities within the Council—these give me hope as well.

The *Call to Action* invites United Methodists to sustained attention to congregational vitality, a focus on leadership development, realigning to support our mission, and reworking the Council of Bishops. These are significant undertakings, and I wrestle with my own impatience on how we shall achieve them.

And yet there are many signs of hope. Picture a heat map, where clusters of fruitful ministry activity are lighted against a dark background with the most fruitful and vital ministries shining brightest. The heat map of The United Methodist Church would allow us to see bright spots in unexpected places, concentrations of vital ministry and congregations that are thriving. Some are in urban areas, some in suburbs, and some in the most isolated rural counties. Africa is aglow with congregational vitality and mission partnerships, but also the map draws our attention to an exceptional campus ministry in one area and to a courageous witness for the homeless in another. A flourishing traditional church lights up near a dynamic merger. Some conferences and seminaries and foundations and agencies glow bright as they risk genuine innovation to realign with the mission. Lights here and there, bright spots appear in places we never expected.

Some rekindling of ministry and reconsideration of mission stretch us uncomfortably, and some innovations don't go far enough. When the church changes, there are thousands of details to argue over if we choose to do so. Or we can look at the big picture, the change in culture and process that redirects the flow toward vital congregations.

We see a new church, and there are signs of it here and there in congregations, conferences, agencies, and at the Council. Something is happening in our church. The Spirit that blows where it will is creating openings for conversation and for a way forward with faithfulness. The way things have been is not the way they will be. And this gives me hope.

Where do you see signs of a new church, of a burgeoning of life through fruitful ministry?

What initiatives and ministries in your congregation, your conference, or the general church give you hope?

Pray through 2 Corinthians 5:17-20 in Eugene Peterson's *THE MESSAGE* for fresh insight from a familiar passage.

What a wildly wonderful world, God. Take up residence in our church afresh, and move us where you would have us go for your purposes. Heal us from dimness of sight and awaken us from dullness of spirit. Open our eyes to the striking power of your grace at work in us and in our congregation. By your Spirit, make us one with Christ, one with each other, and one in service to all the world.

28
Somewhere Out There

Somewhere out there is a five-year-old boy who doesn't know that right now plans are being made by a congregation he's never heard of to offer a neighborhood vacation Bible school that will change the direction of his life. The songs he will sing will stick in his mind, the stories of Jesus will enliven his imagination. The puppet show will make him laugh, the teacher will make him feel loved and welcomed, and the hospitality of those followers of Christ will so touch his mom and dad that they will take a small, unexpected step toward faith.

Somewhere out there is an elderly woman who feels as if everyone has forgotten her. Her world has shrunk to her small apartment, the weekly trips to the grocery store, and the visits to the doctor's office. Her television has become her best friend. She doesn't know it, but right now a nearby congregation has awakened to the calling of God to invite people like her to a weekly lunch and to a chance to serve others. Soon she'll use her long-neglected skills to knit baby blankets that will wrap medical supplies bound for Central America, and this taste of community will save her life and give her a rebirth she never imagined possible.

Somewhere out there in a rural Philippine village, a young couple strive to cope with the unexpected loss of their daughter in a flood that washed away their home. They don't realize it now, but even as they grieve, neighbors are holding them in prayer and asking God for the best way to surround them with the love of Christ. They cannot imagine now how the stories of faith, the songs of worship, and the embrace of strangers will move them step by step toward a sense of life they thought they would never see again.

Somewhere out there is a teacher who thinks no one else cares about the children she has given her life to serving. Her schoolroom is rundown, and there's less money now than ever before to provide the resources she needs to do her job. She has no idea that a congregation is preparing for a new ministry that will change her circumstances. Six months from now she will weep with joy as strangers repaint and refurbish her classroom. She cannot imagine that droves of people will step forward to volunteer to tutor, to read stories, and to coach basketball. She has no inkling of the effect this will have on her and on her students, and how this will open the door by which she rediscovers her own faith in Christ.

Somewhere out there is a young man whose inability to cope with the basic mechanisms of daily living has caused him to lose his job, to stop taking his medication, and to slip through the cracks of every social, community, and family network. He kept falling until now he sleeps on the streets, carries cardboard for bedding, and digs through trash for dinner. He has no idea that a congregation is gearing up to offer a soup kitchen, and that this ministry will change his life. He cannot imagine that as he is served a meal, someone will engage him in conversation, treat him as human, listen to his story, learn his name, and reconnect him to his family and to the social networks that will allow him to live again a basic life with dignity. He has no idea that God, working through people desiring to follow Christ, will restore him to a life he barely remembers.

Somewhere out there in an African village a young girl and her little sister read stories together in bed, both of them safely protected by a mosquito net bought by the youth of a rural church in the American Midwest. No one can see it now, but she will grow up to become a doctor, relieving the suffering of thousands. She will live a full life that never would have been possible without a simple net and many generous young hearts across the globe.

When United Methodists work toward starting congregations and strengthening congregations and leading congregations, these are not merely attempts at institutional survival. Learning to deepen our life in Christ through congregations and to extend the outreach of Christ through faith communities are not merely submitting to worldly, corporate models of growth and success. Forming congregations are a means by which we cooperate with the Holy Spirit in fulfilling the purposes of Christ. Through people changed by belonging to the body of Christ, God transforms the world. God uses congregations to fulfill the mission revealed to us in Christ; increasing the number of vital congregations deserves our best and highest insights, efforts, resources, and attention.

Somewhere out there, somewhere in Texas or California or New Jersey or Norway or Mozambique, somewhere in a town like yours or a neighborhood near you is a person who has no idea of the change that is coming his way or the grace that will transform her life, a person unknowingly prepared by the Spirit of God to receive the embrace of Christ that people will offer when they come alive with purpose and fulfill the mission of Christ.

Somewhere out there is a person God plans to use you to reach. Somewhere out there is a person God will use to change your life as you reach them. Somewhere out there is a person for whom Christ died, and for whom your church was built, and for whom God has uniquely prepared you to reach.

Who are the "somewhere out there" people you and your congregation are reaching?

Has your congregation ever helped start a congregation? How do you, your church, and your conference work to strengthen the ministry of Christ through congregations?

Who are you uniquely qualified and perfectly situated to touch with the grace and ministry of Christ whom no one else can possibly reach?

For further exploration, contemplate I John 3:17-19 from *THE MESSAGE*. What does it mean to suggest that our inaction makes God's love disappear?

Lord, may we not miss the person you have prepared us to reach on your behalf, and not fail the calling you have given us in Christ. Lift our eyes, dear God, and help us look beyond our own small world to a place far away or surprisingly nearby where you call us to make a difference.

Recommended Reading

Congregational Fruitfulness, Change, Church Leadership

Bearing Fruit: Ministry with Real Results, by Lovett Weems and Thomas M. Berlin

Does Your Church Have a Prayer? by Marc Brown, Kathy Merry, and John Briggs

A Door Set Open: Grounding Change in Mission and Hope, by Peter L. Steinke

Direct Hit, by Paul Borden

The Externally Focused Church, by Rick Rusaw and Eric Swanson

Five Practices of Fruitful Congregations, by Robert Schnase

Leading Beyond the Walls: Developing Congregations with a Heart for the Unchurched, by Adam Hamilton

Legacy Churches, by Stephen Gray and Franklin Dumond

Make or Break Your Church in 365 Days, by Paul Borden

The Race to Reach Out, by Doug Anderson and Michael Coyner

Renovate or Die, by Bob Farr and Kay Kotan

Simple Church, by Thom Rainer and Eric Geiger

Visioneering, by Andy Stanley

Reaching New Generations

Almost Christian: What the Faith of Our Teenagers is Telling the American Church, by Kenda Creasy Dean

Lost and Found: The Younger Unchurched and the Churches that Reach Them, by Ed Stetzer

Reaching People under 40 while Keeping People over 60, by E. Hammett and J Pierce

Slow Fade, Reggie Joiner, Chuck Bomar, and Abbie Smith

Tribal Church: Ministering to the Missing Generation, by Carol Howard Merritt

UnChristian: What a New Generation Really Thinks about Christianity, by David Kinnaman and Gabe Lyons

Worlds Apart: Understanding the Mindset & Values of 18-25-year-olds, by Chuck Bomar

Organizational Dynamics and Change
Good to Great, by Jim Collins
Good to Great and the Social Sectors: A Monograph to Accompany Good to Great, by Jim Collins
Leadership on the Line, by Ronald Heifetz
Managing Transitions, by William Bridges
Orbiting the Giant Hairball, by Gordon MacKenzie
Results that Last, by Quint Studer
Switch: How to Change Things When Change is Hard, by Chip and Dan Heath

Discipleship
Finding Our Way Again: The Return of the Ancient Practices, by Brian McLaren
Five Practices of Fruitful Living, by Robert Schnase
Unbinding the Gospel, by Martha Grace Reese

The United Methodist Context for Mission and Change
American Saint: Francis Asbury and the Methodists, by John H. Wigger
Back to Zero: The Search to Rediscover the Methodist Movement, by Gil Rendle
Focus: The Real Challenges That Face the United Methodist Church, by Lovett Weems
Journey in the Wilderness: New Life for Mainline Churches, by Gil Rendle

Notes

Introduction: How to Use This Book
1. From Peter Steinke's book, *A Door Set Open* (Herndon: Alban Institute, 2010), p. 41.

1. Shouts for Joy and the Sounds of Weeping
1. Ronald A. Heifetz and Marty Lindsey, *Leadership on the Line: Staying Alive through the Dangers of Leadership* (Boston: Harvard Business School Press, 2002).
2. John Wesley, *Journal,* April 2, 1739 (Chicago: Moody Press, 1951), also available at http://www.ntslibrary.com/pdf%20Books/Wesley-Journal.pdf

2. The Destination
1. Lovett Weems and Thomas M. Berlin, *Bearing Fruit: Ministry with Real Results* (Nashville: Abingdon, 2011), ch. 3.

3. The Challenge of the Ages
1. *National Geographic,* March 2011, see poster insert.
2. Statistics from 2009 General Council on Finance and Administration report.
3. Wesley Theological Seminary, "Reaching More Diverse People," 2009; www.churchleadership.com/pdfs/DiversityReport2009.pdf

4. Four Thousand Shalls
1. Gordon MacKenzie, *Orbiting the Giant Hairball* (New York: Viking Penguin, 1996).
2. John Wesley, Sermon 17: "Circumcision of the Heart," Jan. 1, 1733, St. Mary's, Oxford.

5. Praying Hands and Dirty Fingernails
1. Mary Atkins, presentation at the 2011 World Methodist Conference in South Africa.

7. Forty Days
1. John Wiggers, *American Saint: Francis Asbury and the Methodists* (New York: Oxford University Press, 2009), 45.

8. Pruning for Growth
1. Drucker advocated the practice of planned abandonment, the concepts of which stemmed from Drucker Foundation employee (and former CEO of Girl Scouts) Francis Hesselbein, author of *Hesselbein on Leadership.*

9. "An Especial Care"
1. Albert Outler, *John Wesley* (New York: Oxford University Press, 1964), 134.
2. A Methodist Preacher, *John Wesley, the Methodist* (New York: Methodist Book Concern, 1903). Accessed on 12 April 2012, http://wesley.nnu.edu/john-wesley/john-wesley-the-methodist/chapter-xiii-inconference-with-the-preschers/
3. Russell E. Richey, *The Methodist Conference in America: A History* (Nashville: Abingdon, 1996).
4. Outler, *John Wesley,* 164.

12. Changing Lives
1. Gil Rendle, *Journey in the Wilderness* (Nashville: Abingdon, 2010), 23.

14. People No One Else Can Reach
1. Adam Hamilton, *Leading Beyond the Walls: Developing Congregations With a Heart for the Unchurched* (Nashville: Abingdon, 2002).

15. Love With Legs
1. John Wesley, Sermon 24, "Upon the Lord's Sermon on the Mount," http://www.new.gbgm-umc-org/umhistory/wesley/sermons/24
2. *Call to Action,* http://www.umc.org/atf/cf/%7Bdb6a45e4-c446-4248-82c8-e131b6424741%7D/EXECUTIVE_SUMMARY_CALL_TO_AC-TION.PDF

21. The Big Rocks
1. Stephen Covey, A. Roger Merril, and Rebecca R. Merril, *First Things First* (London: Simon and Schuster, 1994), 88-89.
2. Robert Schnase, *Five Practices of Fruitful Congregations* (Nashville: Abingdon, 2007).

26. "Laid Aside by Thee"
1. John Wesley, The Covenant Prayer, The United Met*hodist Hymnal* (Nashville: The United Methodist Publishing House, 1989), 607.

28. Somewhere Out There
Adapted from Robert Schnase, *The Balancing Act* (Nashville: Abingdon Press, 2009).

Praise for *Remember the Future: Praying for the Church and Change*

"While Bishop Schnase honors the past, he writes for the future. God keeps doing new things, and our Wesleyan ancestors knew well that new occasions require new responses. *Remember the Future* envisions a future worthy of our past."

Lovett H. Weems, Jr., Wesley Theological Seminary, author of *Focus: The Real Challenges That Face The United Methodist Church*

"This is a necessary tool for leaders. Discerning God's dream for us requires remembering who we are and where we come from. More than making decisions and organizational responsibilities we need help staying connected with God's purpose while working. Here is help."

Gil Rendle, Texas Methodist Foundation Senior Consultant, author of *Journey in the Wilderness* and *Back to Zero*

Quantity Discounts Available.

Praise for *Remember the Future: Praying for the Church and Change*

"The R & B singer and songwriter Sam Cooke did a very popular song entitled 'A Change Is Gonna Come.' Our future in the church depends greatly upon how we face the need for and the opportunity of change. Bishop Schnase helps us to embrace change with faith, vision, hope, and grace. I intend to make wide use of this book in my ministry with congregational leaders."

Gregory V. Palmer, Resident Bishop of the Illinois Area of The United Methodist Church

"The biggest issue facing local churches, annual conferences, synods, dioceses, and the national church is whether we love Jesus enough to change. The kind of faithfulness that brought us here will not serve us well in the future. We must remember the changes our ancestors made and make similar changes to remain faithful in the future. Robert Schnase has given us significant help on that journey."

Scott Jones, Resident Bishop of the Kansas Area of The United Methodist Church

Quantity Discounts Available.